WHAT YOU DON'T KNOW ABOUT PRAYER

WHAT YOU DON'T KNOW ABOUT PRAYER

A Bible Study on the Subject of Prayer

Berean Publications
4459 US Highway 17
Fleming Island, Florida 32003

Published in Fleming Island, Florida, by Berean Publications.

Please pardon our grammar as this book was derived from sermons preached by Dr. Tom Neal. Some grammar rules were overlooked due to keeping the integrity of the meaning of the sermon.

ISBN: 978-0-9771829-5-4

DEDICATION

This book is dedicated to my faithful, loving wife, Becky. For forty-two years, she has been a constant source of encouragment and inspiration for me as I have done my best to be true to my Heavenly calling. Without her by my side, I could not have achieved a faithful testimony.

I would also like to express thanks to the members of Berean Baptist Church who have called me *Preacher* for over twenty-eight years. They have been a constant source of strength and encouragement. Without their help and support, this project would not have been possible.

ACKNOWLEDGEMENT

I would like to thank my son and co-pastor, Greg Neal, for his editing and encouragement in pursuing this endeavour.

I would also like to thank Brian Healy for the ingenious cover design.

Thank you Bob and Arlene Dendy for the editing and layout of this book.

I would also like to thank Pam Triplett and Cindy Healy for their tireless efforts in editing this book.

I am also grateful to Becky Powell for her help in the layout and design of this book.

TABLE OF CONTENTS

PREFACE

During a frustrating period of my life, I asked myself, "If God answers prayer, why are things in such a mess?" I arrived at what I thought was a very logical conclusion; I know that God answers prayer. Consequently, I concluded that the problem was on my end and that I was not really praying as I should.

I am afraid that a vast majority of Christians have become too ritualistic in every area of their spiritual lives. If we are going to have a national revival or even personal one, it is going to take more than preaching, soulwinning, and the latest idea on church building and leadership. It is going to take a sincere humility and realness as we go before God Himself and empty ourselves in prayer. History has shown us that if there is no earnest, heartfelt prayer that loses all concept of time and cost, there will be no revival. Churches will become a facade, and the cost to sinners and our families will be unfathomable.

During my lifetime, I have had the privilege of praying with great men of prayer such as Hyman Appleman, R.G. Lee, J. Harold Smith, Lee Roberson, John Rice, Jack Hyles, and many other saints of God. As I reflect on these men and their dedication to a true life of prayer, I become convicted of my own ineffective prayer life. Therefore, my desire in these messages is to motivate myself to have a real and effective prayer life and to help others to be bold enough to enter the throne room of our Heavenly Father with earnest petitions that would bring an answer from Heaven.

CHAPTER 1

The Sin of Prayerlessness

I Samuel 12:22-23 says, *For the LORD will not forsake his people for his great name's sake: because it hath pleased the LORD to make you his people. Moreover as for me, God forbid that I should sin against the LORD in ceasing to pray for you.* Notice that Samuel does not say it is a sin against the individual if he does not pray for others. He said it is a sin against the Lord if he does not pray for the people. If we do not pray for each other, it is sin. The Bible is very clear on this. Verse 23 concludes, *but I will teach you the good and the right way.*

Let us look at the sin of prayerlessness. There is no way that we can deny the fact that prayer is a divine command of God. Prayer is also a human necessity. The greatest privilege that you and I have is to be able to enter into the very presence of God and to make our requests known unto Him. The Bible says that to neglect the performance of this command of God is sin. Have you heard any sermons about the sin of prayerlessness? Most of the time, we hear preaching about many topics other than prayer. I believe that this is due to the fact that most people are very weak in the matter of prayer.

This sin of prayerlessness is a sin of which we hear very little. This sin is seldom taken to heart or given concern. Most people would say that they do not pray every day. Some do not really spend much time in prayer at all. They act as if it is no big deal. Most people do not pray an hour a week. Most of us are defeated in this area of our lives, and we do not take it to heart. Many are not even upset about their lack of prayer. That is why we need to ask God, first of all, to forgive us because we have all come short in the matter of prayer. I do not know of one person who could say that he knows that he has spent the time in prayer that God would have him to spend.

We are commanded by God to pray. To not pray is a sin of omission. All of our lives, we have heard of the sins of omission and commission. Prayerlessness is a sin of omission. The sins of omission are very subtle because they do not bring any immediate alarm or guilt to our lives.

Are there people's lives who have been helped because of your prayers? Are there people who have avoided tragedy because of your prayers? Are there people whose needs have been supplied because of your prayers? If we are honest when we look at ourselves, I think that we all need to get to the altar. We need to learn how to pray. The disciples said to

Jesus, "Teach us to pray." They did not say, "Teach us how to preach like you preach, Jesus." They did not say, "Jesus, teach us how to heal people like you heal people." They asked one thing—teach us to pray like You prayed. Oh, that we might get a hunger to want to pray.

Sometimes it is said to people, "You have plenty of time. You could be a prayer warrior. You could really pray." These people then look at you with a puzzled look. Many times we think that the only way we serve God today is by being a jack rabbit, doing something at ninety miles an hour, or being where we get some acclaim. The real work of God is done through prayer and the real power of God comes from prayer. Oh, how we need to learn to pray today!

There are several things that happen when we sin and do not pray as we should. We know that all sin has consequences. We very seldom think of the ramifications of the sin of prayerlessness. Let us look at some of these repercussions.

First, not praying invokes the fury of God against us. Jeremiah 10:25 says, *Pour out thy fury upon the heathen that know thee not, and upon the families that call not on thy name.* Do you see what the Bible says? God's fury will be poured out on the families that do not call on His name. Does your family call on the name of God? Does your family regularly call on His name stating your family's needs and calling on Him to meet them? The Bible says that not doing so can invoke the fury of God upon your home and family. There are enough things opposing us in this world without having God against us also. The Bible says that if we do not call on God, He will invoke His fury. No sin provokes God like the sin of idolatry. We read about God's jealousness and His hatred towards idolatry, but there is no insult to God like the sin of ignoring Him. When we ignore God, it is an insult because we are saying we are self-sufficient; we are our own god; we can provide for our own needs.

One of the great sins of prayerlessness is that you are not acknowledging to God that you need Him. You are not acknowledging Who He is, you are not honoring Him for being Who He is. You are not letting God know that you realize that everything you have here on earth comes from Him. Calling on the name of God is something everyone can do and needs to do because we are all dependent upon His faithfulness. You are not self-made. You did not put yourself in that house in which you live. You did not put yourself in that car that you drive. You did not put those clothes on your body, or that food in your pantry. There is a God in Heaven. If it were not for His mercy, His grace, and His faithfulness, you would not be who you are or have what you have. Christians are in serious trouble today because many are running around like self-sufficient gods, not acknowledging God Who gives them everything. Sadly, His fury is going to be upon us.

Without God, we are nothing. Without Him, we can do nothing of eternal value. God is grieved when He is disregarded. We must call upon Him and not ignore Him. When God answers our prayers, He saves and blesses us. However, when we do not pray, we hinder God from blessing us. If I do not pray for someone and that person for whom I do not pray could have been saved by my prayer, helped by my prayer, or strengthened by my prayer, I am inviting God's fury!

There are people for whom you ought to pray. Samuel said, *God forbid that I should sin against the LORD in ceasing to pray for you.* If I do not pray for you and something happens to you that my prayer could have prevented, the Bible says the fury of God will be unleashed against me. I do not like hearing that. There is too much at stake for us not pray. We need to realize what the Bible says about prayer. He pours out His fury on those who are guilty of the sin of prayerlessness.

Secondly, not praying is a sin of omission. James 4:17 says, *Therefore to him that knoweth to do good, and doeth it not, to him it is sin.* Prayer is doing a good thing that leads to the doing of many more good things. To abstain from praying will eventually lead to doing wrong because of a lack of courage. Prayer gives us the courage that we need to keep us from doing wrong and enables us to do right. The sin of omission is the failure to do good when we know we should do good. Sins of omission are very deceitful because they seemingly bring no condemnation, guilt, shame, sorrow, or conviction. That is why these sins are so easy to commit. Very few people come down the aisle and say that they are convicted of any of the above.

What does convict you? Are you convicted because you know you are not doing all you should do? Perhaps you may think that somebody else will pray. Maybe your excuse is that you just ran out of time or that God understands. People generally say that they are convicted because they did this or said that. That is good, but what about the things that you are leaving undone that you are supposed to do? The things that we do not do leave no alarm; therefore, many omit and keep on omitting these sins because they feel that it does no harm. Yet, it is a sin in the sight of God. It does not matter whether you feel convicted or not. Not praying is sin!

Many people today wonder why they are living under the fury and anger of God. I will tell you why—you are omitting something that is very important. You are not praying and do not have a prayer life. Prayer is the way we get God's work done, and not praying is a sin of omission.

Thirdly, not praying leads to spiritual poverty. James 4:2 says, *...ye have not, because ye ask not.* It is very simple. God says you do not have it because you did not ask for it. How many more things would we have today if we had a regular time of prayer where we really prayed and poured out our hearts to

God and asked for what we needed? How many wonderful things could He do for us! God said, *Call unto me, and I will answer thee, and I will shew thee great and mighty things, which thou knowest not.* God says, "You call and I show." He does not say, "I show and then you call." He says, *Call unto me.* If we call unto Him, He will show us things we did not know. We live like spiritual paupers. God does not want us to live that way. He has provided many things for us that we do not get because we simply do not ask for them.

Praying, Bible reading, and doing God's work feeds, strengthens, and builds up the inner man. The reason some people are strong is that they have a spiritual life of spending time in prayer, reading their Bible, and doing the work of God. These areas will strengthen the inner man. Failing to do these things leads to spiritual impoverishment, making our inner man weak. Our faith becomes weak, our life becomes weak, and our spiritual strength becomes weak. We become spiritual defeatists when we do not feed that inner man. A strong Christian starts with having a prayer life. When you see a weak Christian, you are looking at someone who does not pray.

Many people go around saying, "I pray. I pray." The reality is that they do not! The Bible says that if you regard iniquity in your heart, the Lord will not hear you. It does not matter who you are or who you know. It does not matter how much money you have. If you have sin in your life, you are not praying. That is why God gave us I John 1:9. We have religious people saying that they pray, but they do not. Your life shows that you are a spiritual pauper, and you are trying to convince me that you pray? It is time to be realistic. Revival and victory come through prayer. Everything that we need comes through prayer.

There is no joy or triumph in the life of a prayerless person. When a person is not what he should be, it is because of prayerlessness. Sometimes we look at a person and say, "That is the result of being with the wrong person at the wrong place." Actually, it is the result of being somebody who does not spend time with God, who does not walk and fellowship with God, who does not call upon God, and who does not depend upon God. That is the reason we sin. That is the reason we fail. If we have no spiritual walk with God, we have no strength.

When a person is not what he should be, it is most often because of prayerlessness. That person is doing an injustice to himself, to God, and to those around him who need his help. There are people who need your help but who will never get it because you do not pray. Buy all the toys and games you want. Go on all the vacations you want, but if you cannot pray for your family, you are not doing anything for them. Oh, how sad that the fury of God is blowing through our houses and lives only because we refuse to have the prayer life that we are supposed to have with God!

It is impossible to please God, to be a help to others, or to live a victorious life without prayer. When I think of this thought, I am convicted in my heart. I hope that this convicts you as well. The only hope we have in this world is to learn to pray. The only hope this country has is God's people learning to pray again. The only hope we have is quitting this little religious game we all play and get real with God. We need to get on our faces before the almighty God and pour our hearts out, claiming what He has for us. We need to quit thinking that prayer is not that important. We cannot have revival if we do not pray.

Fourthly, not praying allows defeat to come to others. Exodus 17:11-13 says, *And it came to pass, when Moses held up his hand, that Israel prevailed: and when he let down his hand, Amalek prevailed. But Moses' hands were heavy; and they took a stone, and put it under him, and he sat thereon; and Aaron and Hur stayed up his hands, the one on the one side, and the other on the other side; and his hands were steady until the going down of the sun. And Joshua discomfited Amalek and his people with the edge of the sword.* What we do or fail to do always involves God's effect on others. You may think that you are not affecting anyone, but the Bible says that you are. The Bible also teaches you that God's effect on others is regulated by what you do. I can determine somebody's happiness, somebody's future, or somebody's blessed state with God. The victory and success of others are dependent upon our prayers. That is how God made us. You must realize that your wife is dependent upon your prayers. Your husband is dependent upon your prayers. Your children are dependent upon your prayers. Through your prayers, God is going to bless and help others. That is the way God intended it to be. He made us to pray for each other.

Many have suffered defeat, and many have never been saved because someone failed to pray for them. Ponder this thought for a moment. People can die and go to Hell because you do not pray for them. We do not believe that, but that is what the Bible says. A person who could have succeeded in life will fail because somebody did not pray for him. In this portion of Scripture, we see the power of intercession, the success which comes to others through our prayers, and the defeat that may come to others because of a lack of prayer. Moses intercedes; Joshua triumphs. Moses ceased; the Amalakites triumphed. When Moses was assisted by Aaron and Hur, Joshua prevailed.

If those whom God has called to be leaders and has called to the front lines do not succeed, many will fail to be saved and others will be defeated. Someone who fails to pray can steal someone else's victory. We must realize that, when this happens, much of the responsibility rests on those who failed to pray for their leaders and failed to pray for those people in action for God. We hear about leaders who fail, and we say, "That is so sad. I didn't see that coming." Do I dare ask how much you have prayed for them? Do you pray for your church staff? Do you have their names on your prayer lists, and do you pray for them every day? Do you pray for your pastor? Do you pray for the deacons of your church? Do you pray for your Sunday School teachers? It is time to look in the mirror and realize that the reason some people fail is that Christians do not pray for them. God designed us in such a way that our successes in life are tied to people praying for us. Our successes and our triumphs in life are tied to someone caring enough to pray for us. No one makes himself. No one can create himself. We are all dependent upon God and dependent upon others. Rather than recognize this, we often choose to whine about things instead of changing them. We must come to the place of realizing that others suffer because we fail to pray.

Fifthly, prayerlessness is a sin of neglect. In I Samuel 12:28, the Bible tells us that it would be a sin if we do not pray for others. Samuel knew that victory and success were contingent on his prayers. That is how we ought to live. You know what Samuel is saying in this passage of Scripture? He is saying, "God is not going to forsake you because I am going to pray. I am going to make sure we are okay because I am praying." It would make a difference if you would look at people and say, "I am going to pray for them until they reach success. I am going to pray for them until they come to church. I am going to pray for them until they find the will of God. I am going to pray for my children until they reach the right frame of mind and the right spirit.

We have all these impossible situations because we are living a life of sin—we are living in a prayerless state. Oh, that someone would take the challenge as Samuel did and say, "I am going to make a difference!" Make a difference in a teenager's life. Make a difference in a child's life. If you know people who are going through trials, you should pray for them. We see so many sad and helpless situations everyday, yet we neglect the God given opportunity to pray for them.

As a pastor, so many people have come to me with broken lives and broken hearts, and I have no human answer. However, I can say one thing to them. I can tell them, "I will get on my face before God for you, and I will do my best to pray that your family gets back together. I will pray for your home and for your family's needs." Many times we say that God does answer prayer; however, few of us will pray so that God can do it. We ought to live as if people cannot live without our prayers. You ought to have an attitude toward the people you love and admire that says, "I have to pray for them because they can't make it if I don't pray for them." Samuel did not become guilty of the sin of neglect by ceasing to pray for Israel. When we do not pray, we commit the horrible sin of neglect.

Sixthly, not praying is disobedience to God's commands. Jesus said in Luke 18:1, *Men ought always to pray, and not to faint.* I Timothy 2:8 says, *I will therefore that men pray every where.* All of God's commands are for our good and are not to be neglected. Many will suffer if we neglect them. The person who prays will get a two-fold blessing. First, he is obeying God. Secondly, his prayer will be answered. What a great blessing! The person who does not pray will disobey the Lord, therefore forfeiting the blessing of the Lord. He will also be responsible for the failure of someone else because he does not pray. Many times we resort to crying and whining, but we do not pray. Prayer is the answer. We say it, but do we believe it? What prayer has God answered for you in the last week? What prayer has God answered for you in the last year? If God answers prayer, then why are things in our lives so awful? The truth of the matter is that we do not pray as we should. We all too often fail to spend the time we ought to in prayer.

Seventhly, the sin of prayerlessness can lead to damnation. Romans 10:13 says, *For whosoever shall call upon the name of the Lord shall be saved.* The prayer for salvation is one prayer that you need to be sure you have prayed. After you realized that you were a sinner and owed a debt for your sins and that Jesus' precious blood paid the price for your sins, you cried out to God for mercy and asked Him to forgive you of your sin. By faith, you received that payment for your sin. If you are not saved, then you do not have a prayer life because you cannot pray. You must have a mediator. This mediator is Jesus Christ. If you are not saved, you are helpless and hopeless; and you have no power to change things. If you are saved, you do not have to be helpless. You can have the power of God on your life. Oh, what a great privilege it is to be able to enter into the presence of God and to bring Him our needs and know that He hears us! Do not let your prayerlessness lead to damnation.

Do you know for sure you are saved? If you know that you are saved, prayerlessness is a sin in which you need to win the victory. Forget about all the little things that Christians argue about. If prayer changes things, then why is your life as it is? If prayer changes things, then why is your family in the condition that it is in? If prayer changes things, why are you facing so many things with no hope? There will not be a revival in a nation until there is a revival in the lives of individuals. If we cannot have faith in God to change us, how can we have faith in God to change our country? The sin of prayerlessness is a great sin. If I regard iniquity in my heart, the Lord will not hear me.

Christians need to quit pretending that they pray. If you were asked when your prayer time is, would you have an answer? Prayer is the most important tool we have, and we do not use it. When is your communion time with God? When is your fellowship with God? When is the time that you pour out your heart to God? When is the time you take your friends and family members to God? Do not wait until your chilren get old to pray for them. When they are little babies, take them to God. When they are toddling around, take them to God. When they are teenagers, take them to God. You need to start now! You may think that nobody cares, and no one can help your situation, but there is One Who can.

It is amazing how much prayer, or the lack of it, is tied to so many other things in life. I would like to challenge you to confess the sin of prayerlessness. Confess the sin of not having the right prayer life. Let us really see God do something with our prayer lives. Let us choose something that we are going to change and see if God can do it.

There are so many victories that we can have if we just simply say, "Master, we have a request." Jesus acknowledged His disciples. They did not say, "Teach us to preach like you do." They did not say, "Teach us to heal like you heal." They said, "Would you please teach us how to pray?" Oh, if that would be our hunger when we open our Bible for devotions. He could teach us how to pray for our children, our spouse, and our friends. So much goes undone because we do not know how to pray. May God help us to make prayer an important part of our daily walk with Him so that we would not be found guilty of the sin of prayerlessness.

CHAPTER 2

The High Cost of Prayer

Another prayer promise is given in the Bible. I John 3:22 says, *And whatsoever we ask, we receive of him, because we keep his commandments, and do those things that are pleasing in his sight.* If we ask, we will receive because there is always a cause and effect. If we keep His commandments, and do those things that are pleasing in His sight, He will show His pleasure by answering our prayers. We ought to study the Bible to learn as much as we can about God's promises concerning answered prayer. We should then claim all that we have learned.

Prayer is not a menial task. It is a very important command of God, and it is not a small task. One of the most taxing things a person can do is really pray. Jesus prayed, and He sweat great drops of blood. If you spend time with agony in your heart and soul, it will be very taxing and tiring. That is why our flesh rebels at prayer so much.

Anything worthwhile is costly. If something does not cost much, then it is not worth much. Anything that is any good in life costs us something. We have to work for things of value. If we do not have to strive to attain them, we do not appreciate them as we should. Remember, an article will have a higher cost if it has a greater value.

The reason most people do not have a prayer life is that they are not willing to pay the price. It is costly, but it is valuable. You may think that in order to start praying, you have to get your life right. You may believe that you need to start praying and never do it because you are not willing to pay the price. Christians want to pray until they find out how much it cost. Allow me to be very honest with you. I want to tell you that prayer is going to cost you. Some Christians come to the conclusion that if it is going to cost that much, then they just cannot do it. They will want somebody else to pray for them. No! Nobody can do your praying for you. Nobody can do your soul winning for you. Nobody can do your Bible reading for you. Nobody can live the Christian life for you. You must do it yourself, and it will cost you something. There is a price to pay to serve the Lord. That is the way God intended it to be. Allow me to share several things that prayer will cost you.

First, prayer will cost time. There has to be a time allotted for prayer because it takes time to pray. Sometimes we will need to pray for a long period before we feel that God has heard us or that we have gotten our prayers through all the opposition. Christians need to remember that there is opposition as we pray. We have the opposition of the demons of Hell who oppose our prayer life and oppose answers to our prayers. It requires time to begin to pray. It requires time to get into the spirit of prayer, to get under the burden of prayer, to continue in prayer, and to pray until our answers come through.

When you first start praying, determining what to do is not a great exercise because the Bible lays out how we are to pray. We are to start with praise. It is not scriptural to just start with your wants. The disciples asked of Jesus, "How do we pray?" He began with, *Our Father, which art in Heaven.* Jesus gave God a new name: Our Father, Our Daddy. Jesus then said, *Hallowed be thy name.* You start by praising Him because you need to praise Him and honor Him awhile. It gets His attention; but more importantly, it also focuses your attention as you begin to praise the Lord.

Then the Bible tells us that when we pray, we are to pray for our daily bread. We are to pray for today's bread—not tomorrow's bread, just your daily bread, your daily supply. You are not supposed to pray for everything in the future; you are supposed to pray for your daily needs. You would then follow by praying for forgiveness of your sins, and then you would pray for others.

Most of your time should be spent praying for other people. If we follow Biblical guidelines, we will be spending a substantial amount of time in prayer. We know that the Bible says that time is precious and God-given. The most important thing you have is time because you are only allotted a certain amount in your life. Once you use it up, it is never to be given back or used again. Therefore, in each situation that I invest my time, I should invest it in the most precious commodity that I have. What better way could I invest my time than in prayer to God?

We all invest our time in something. We all find time to do what we need to do. There is no excuse for saying, "Well, I don't have time to pray." You are commanded to pray. You are commanded to take time for prayer. We must realize that prayer is going to cost us time and that we must redeem the time. The best way to redeem our time is to spend it in prayer. Prayer will cost us time, but it will be a worthy investment. Every minute that we devote to prayer will bring Godly returns. Many times we invest our time in something of which we are very excited, but we know that there is not going to be any return for it. We have experienced everything that there was to experience with this excitement, but that is not the case with prayer.

When we pray, we are investing our time wisely, and it courts the favor and blessing of God and restrains the progress of sin. How can we restrain the progress of sin in our lives, homes, and society, as well as restrain it from attacking our children? How can we stop Satan? There is only one way—

by prayer. We must pray. It is urgent that we pray. We must get ahold of God. We will gain much by spending more time in prayer. When we pray, we accomplish much more than when we do not pray. Much time is lost by a lack of prayer. We say we do not have time, but we are losing our time. We are losing the battle by not praying.

The first challenge after realizing that it is going to take time to pray is setting aside a time to pray. It could be a different time for you than it is for me. David said that he prayed three times a day. If you pray three times a day, that fulfills the outline God gave for prayer. The Bible also teaches that we should pray for others at inconvenient times. Have you ever spent a night praying when other people were sleeping? Have you ever spent a night walking around your house, praying for your children while they slept and praying for God to protect them and take care of them? At times like these, you can also pray for friends and others that the Lord puts on your heart. Many times, the greatest accomplishments in prayer come from praying during the most inconvienent times.

Secondly, prayer will cost you strength and energy. Intense and fervent praying is hard work. It costs us energy because prayer is a pouring out of our hearts and of our lives. God intended prayer to be work. Prayer costs us mental energy and strength. You have this time of thinking and meditating upon the things of God that takes mental and physical energy. Prayer might mean giving up some sleep or getting up earlier in the day. While in prayer, we are continually spending our spiritual energy and strength.

When we get into the real stages of prayer in our lives, we will discover that there is not only a spending but also a taking in. There is a difference between a tired body and a tired spirit. We actually re-energize ourselves by prayer, and it will be worthwhile because we will receive a spiritual recuperation even though our physical energy is spent. Your physical body may get tired, but your spirit can be refreshed. The reason most people have a dead, defeated, and tired spirit is that they do not spend time in prayer.

Many people have tired bodies because they are not wise with their time. We can have a tired spirit because we do not pray right. We can do without sleep; but, if we pray, we are going to be energized by the Spirit and the power of God. What you need more than eight hours of sleep is the power of the Holy Spirit in your life. The power of the Holy Spirit is able to overcome anything—any physical calamity and any physical weakness. He can supply anything that we need.

We must realize that if we are going to pray and not sin against the Lord, we must make time to pray. We must give energy and strength to our prayer lives. We must give ourselves to prayer.

Can you fall asleep while you are praying? Some say that they do. No, they do not! What did Jesus say to the disciples when He found them asleep? Did he say, "Oh, did you fall asleep praying?" No! He asked, "What, could you not watch with me one hour?" He did not commend them and say, "Oh, you poor guys. You fell asleep praying." No, they did not fall asleep praying. They fell asleep in a religious exercise. They fell asleep trying to appear religious. When we get into the full energy of prayer, it is going to cost us something; but, at the same time it costs us, it is going to be rejuvenating our spirits.

Thirdly, prayer will cost persecution. How will it cost persecution? We face persecution because prayer will not go unchallenged by Satan. He says that he is going to oppose us. When you get on your knees and start praying, Satan is going to try to stop you. When you get in your prayer closet, he is going to be upset. He is going to try to do everything that he can to stop you. He is going to persecute you. Persecutions, oppositions, and hindrances will come from Satan, worldly people, and even uncommitted Christians. They will not understand that you want to take the time to pray. They will criticize you for prayer. They will do things to hinder your prayer life. There will come an inward conflict, inward struggle, and onslaught from satanic forces. There will be hatred, opposition, and sneering from sinners; and persecution, ridicule, and misunderstanding from non-praying church members. In spite of all of this, it will still pay to pray.

You are going to have opposition when you make up your mind to pray. All you have to do is say, "Dear God, I promise You that I am going to pray," and name a time. I promise you that you are going to start having problems. Perhaps the time that you set to pray is the best time of the day for you. It will not stay that way because Satan will do everything that he can do to stop you from praying. He will do this because the only way to defeat Satan is through prayer. The only way to hold him back is by prayer. The only way not to be defeated by Satan is through prayer. When you decide to pray, you are putting yourself on the front line in the spiritual battle that goes on in this world, and Satan is going to consider you to be someone who needs to be attacked.

It is not mentioned enough that Satan hates you. He would destroy you if he could. His imps are everywhere. He is the prince and the power of the air, and he is all around us. In an unseen world, there is a battle raging. The forces of God are in conflict with the forces of Hell, and we are in this battle. We are supposed to be soldiers in the army, and our main job is to pray. When Satan sees you praying, he becomes angry; and he is going to attack you. He will do all he can to destroy you, but let me encourage you to pray on. It will be worth it. Yes, it is going to take time. Yes, it is going to take strength. Yes, you are going to face enduring persecution. You might even face problems in your life that never existed before you started praying because a prayer life comes with a price tag.

Many times unfortunate circumstances take place in our lives, and we may wonder, "What am I doing wrong?" Many times it is not what we are doing wrong but what we are doing right. That is the reason why persecution comes. That is why troubles and trials come—because of what we are doing right. If you do not have any burdens or trials and the world is not picking on you and Satan is not bothering you, it is probably because you are not doing a mighty work for God.

Fourthly, prayer will cost humility. Humility is a very rare virtue. The Bible says that we must humble ourselves. A person cannot be effective in his prayer life when pride is in his heart.

God will not hear a person who has pride in his heart. God resists those that are proud. If you pray when you are full of pride, what do you think that God will do? He will resist your prayer, and He will not acknowledge it. The Bible says that you can be in such poor spiritual shape that your prayer can become an abomination to God. God resists the prayers of proud people; therefore, we must humble ourselves in order to pray efficiently and effectively. We must humble ourselves before God because God promised to give grace to the humble.

In the past, someone illustrated this point in this way: God has two arms. He has a left hand, which in the Bible is referred to as His mighty hand that is over us. His right arm is considered His everlasting arm, and it is underneath us. God uses the hand that He needs to touch us. We are commanded to submit ourselves under the mighty hand, the left hand of God. If we exalt ourselves and we rise up to that hand, it is that hand that God will use to chasten us and bring us down. If you start thinking that you are a good Christian, God is going to show you that you are not. If you think that you have this life conquered and you do not need prayer, God will show you that you do. He puts you in your place with His left hand, the mighty hand of God. When we humble ourselves, we come down to that right hand of God, that mighty arm that God uses to exalt us. He will then lift us up.

If you feel as if you cannot get ahead or that your prayers are going no farther than the ceiling or if you keep trying to serve God and everything just keeps going wrong, then I can tell you what your problem is. God has His hand on top of you, and He is pushing you down. He is pushing you down because He resists the proud. If you will humble yourself before God and do the best that you can, you will be saying, "I don't understand this; why are all these good things happening to me?" God has lifted you up! He lifts you up when you humble yourself. He pushes you down when you exalt yourself. That is a wonderful truth to understand.

Humility is the way to exaltation and promotion. Humility moves the hand of God to do things for us as we entreat Him. It pays to humble ourselves before God in prayer, but it is going to take a humbling on your part. You are going to have to realize that you can do nothing on your own.

No one ever spoke on prayer and moved me as much as Dr. John Rice. He used to say that prayer was simply asking. He was right. Prayer is asking! We have our own opinions of prayer, but it boils down to one thing—prayer is asking. We have to ask God for something. As a pastor, I have had Christians say to me, "I feel bad because I'm always asking God." What else can you do? Is there anything that you can give God? What does He need from you? We have to ask God for something. By asking Him, we are saying, "You have everything, and I have nothing. I need You, God!" We must ask God. We must understand and comprehend this fact. You must humble yourself to the point that you realize that you have to ask God. Prayer is asking. The Bible tells us to ask over and over again. Ask, and ye shall receive. Ye have not, because ye ask not.

We must come to the place in our lives of humbling ourselves to the point of admitting that we need help. Some people have the attitude that they are not going to let anybody help them. This gets them into trouble with God. It causes the left hand of God to smack them down. We need to understand that God sometimes puts us in situations where we are going to have to accept help from humanity. This help from humanity is God's way of helping us, and God wants us to be humble about it. You may think that you are not the kind of person that lets people help you, but God can force you to be that kind of person. God can put you into a place where you will not survive unless you ask Him for something. We must learn to ask God.

Fifthly, if we progress in our prayer life, it will require soul agony. Prayer must become the soul's sincere desire, uttered or unexpressed. We have to learn to pray from our soul, our inner being. The Bible says that the Holy Spirit is our prayer partner Who helps us with groanings which cannot be uttered. The Holy Spirit will actually pray on our behalf and take our needs and wishes to God when we cannot express them out of the depth of our souls. That is why prayer is directly tied to being filled with the Spirit of God. If you are going to be successful, you must have the Holy Spirit's help.

Everyone who has prayed earnestly before the Lord knows that we can always pray best when we carry a large burden. We do not pray well without a burden. We do not pray well without pressure. Pressure is your friend because pressure makes you realize how weak you are. Pressure makes you realize that you cannot do it yourself and that you need help. Pressure forces you to run to God.

Soul agony comes when our hearts long for something, or we have inward agony because of burdens, leading us to agonizing prayer. When the soul is thus moved to agony, it moves God. God does not get moved by flowery words. God does not get moved because you have a certain knowledge of Him and knowledge of the Bible. What moves God is the broken-hearted, sobbing soul of man that cries out in desperation to Him. That moves God!

What hinders some people from getting their prayers answered is that they are not desperate. It is as if they think that there is another way to solve life's problems, but there is no other way. We must get this soul agony in our prayer life. When our souls are moved to agony, it moves God. Then God will change our conditions, change our circumstances, and change people.

"Now I lay me down to sleep" is not going to do much good for you. When you pray, you ought to experience every emotion. There ought to be an agony of your soul that drains everything out of you and causes you to cry out in despair to God. That is what God wants from us. This is when He will change our circumstances.

At Gethsemane, Christ prayed with soul agony. It expressed itself in humility and submission. If we read the history of the great Christians of our times, we find that they were men who were given to prayer. They prayed in agony of soul and prayed as if they were in a trance. They even prayed for days at a time.

Authors tell us that George Whitfield, the great evangelist, would go into the woods to pray, and nobody would hunt while he was there because there was such an eerie feeling in the woods. This power was felt because of that man's agony of soul and his begging God for revival. People could not stay in the woods. They had to leave.

It was said that Charles Finney could walk down the streets of a town and men would run out of saloons and fall at his feet and beg God for mercy. After spending time praying and walking with God in the woods, Charles Finney could walk into a factory, and the whole factory would come to a stop. Men would begin to weep and cry because there was a man who had given himself so much to God and had so much soul agony for people's lives that God honored it with a supernatural power.

We hear things like this, and we are amazed. David Brainerd literally prayed and preached himself to death before he was thirty years of age because of his burden for the American Indians. I have read that there were times when these people would come to kill him, and they would be restrained because they would see an army with him. There was no army with him. He was all by himself. He would be on his knees, praying in agony of soul. He gave his life with a burden for the American Indians. He did it with such passion and with such agony that God honored his efforts.

We could go on to talk about others: William Carey, John Knox, and George Muller, to name a few. They all possessed soul agony in prayer, which moved God so much that He hearkened unto them and gave them their hearts' desire. Such soul burdens were begotten by the Holy Spirit. That is why you have to have a relationship with God's Holy Spirit—a spiritual relationship. These great men unburdened themselves before God in prayer, and He brought to fruition their holy desires. We must strive for a soul agony in prayer; for, in the end, that agony will bring great joy to God and to us.

There are some prayers that should be so important to you that they are literally agonizing to pray. It is agonizing for you to face the needs of a loved one or a child. It may be a situation that breaks your heart at the mere thought of it. You try to recoil from the needs, and you do not want to face them. What you need to do is get into a mindset of prayer and begin agonizing with God. Suffer the pain, suffer the loss of strength, and agonize your soul so that God might be moved on your behalf.

Sixthly, a prayer life will cost seclusion and loneliness. If a person never desires to be alone with God, that person does not know much about praying. To become efficient in prayer, we must have a desire to be alone with God in prayer. We must desire seclusion and a secret closet where we can be alone with Him. There are times when it is good for people to pray together. The Bible says that where two or three are gathered together in His name, He is in the midst of them. On certain issues in life, it is good to pray that way; but the mightiest answers to prayer come from praying alone with God. That is why we are told in the Bible to enter into our closets so that nobody can see or hear us. This type of prayer is shear agony between you and God, and you do not involve other people in it. You enter into your closet bringing forth loneliness. The most mighty prevailing prayer is done in the secret closet.

Let us look at some Biblical illustrations of this point. Jacob was not a person of character. He was a deceiver. His word did not mean much until that one night he spent alone with God. The liar and deceiver had a name change overnight. He received a new name of a prince. That was a painful night, and he came out of it crippled. He never had been anything before this encounter with God. He got alone with God one night, and the Bible says that he wrestled with God. Jacob would not let go of God until He blessed Him. God likes it when we refuse to take no for an answer. God likes it when we do not let Him go. Just like Jacob, God may have to cripple us. Just like Jacob, we should be willing to say, "OK, then cripple me! I may walk with a limp, but I will walk with the power of God. I may walk with a limp, but I will walk with the reputation of which I am proud." Jacob was changed in one night, and we can be too.

David was changed in a night. David lived alone in the caves, and God changed him. He became the sweet singer of Israel. David, a vagabond that stood underneath the stars all alone, became the one after God's own heart.

John the Baptist did not have much of a social life. He would suddenly appear just as Elijah did. Have you ever noticed that the great men of the Bible suddenly appear out of nowhere? Where had they been? They had been with God. They had been praying. They had been out in a cave somewhere, or out in the woods somewhere. They had been somewhere with God, and suddenly God gave them what they needed. He gave them a message, and then they appeared.

When they came, it was obvious that they were noticed. Nobody could ignore John the Baptist when he came. Nobody could ignore Elijah when he showed up. These were men who had been alone with God. It was obvious that they had been with God, that they were from God, and that they were of God.

Do you have your secret place? Enter into that secret place and pray, and the Bible says that the Father will reward you openly and publicly. Do you have a place where you can go to get alone? It is fine to pray when you drive. It is fine to live in an attitude of prayer, but there are some prayers that must take place in your secret place. There are some events in life that you cannot pray for behind the steering wheel. There are some events in life that you cannot pray for as you take a few minutes for a walk. There are some events in life where we have to have an agony of soul, where we have to be alone with God, and where we have to have God do something for us. You sometimes need to have a prayer meeting where God shakes you. We ought to be shaken because of prayer.

Seventhly, prayer will cost you yourself. A person cannot be successful and at his best in his prayer life if he holds anything in reserve or if there is any part of him not fully consecrated to the Lord. So much of our spiritual life is tied to prayer. You have to be fully consecrated to God. You have to be sold out for the Lord. The person who prays efficiently must be completely yielded to the Lord and hold himself open to be the answer to his own prayer.

The Lord told His disciples to pray. He wanted them to pray, but He did not tell them to pray for sinners. The Bible does not really say to pray for sinners. For what did Jesus tell them to pray? *Pray ye therefore the Lord of the harvest, that he will send forth labourers into his harvest.* He also says, *as my Father hath sent me, even so send I you.* The point that I am making is do not pray a prayer if you are not willing to be the answer to your prayer. Sometimes we want God to do everything, but God is going to show us how we can do it ourselves. Do not pray unless you are willing to be the instrument that God uses to answer your prayer. When Jesus sent the disciples forth, He answered their prayer.

William Carey, the great missionary and forefather of the Baptist faith, received a burden for the world and began to pray for the conversion of the world. He asked everyone to join with him in prayer for the world. It ended up costing him and the others who prayed very much because they surrendered themselves. God answered William Carey's prayer by sending him to the mission field.

No one can pray earnestly, fervently, passionately, consistently, and persistently, and withhold his labor, time, money, or life. If you are going to pray about something, you need to be willing to be the instrument. If you are going to pray for somebody's financial needs, be willing to be the instrument to answer that prayer. If you are going to pray for somebody who needs a friend, be ready to be the friend. If you are going to pray for missionaries on the field, be willing to be the answer to the prayer. That is the only way God is going to bless your prayer life.

CHAPTER 3

The Fruits of a Successful Prayer Life

Mark 11:24 says, *Therefore I say unto you, What things soever ye desire, when ye pray, believe that ye receive them, and ye shall have them.*

God has ordained that everything should increase and bring forth after its own kind. That is the plan of God in creation. That is the plan of God today. Above all other things, every Christian should bring forth fruit after his kind. There are two kinds of fruit each Christian should bear: the fruit of being and the fruit of doing.

Everyone who is truly born again should have the fruit of being—being a Christian and being what a Christian should be. He should also bear the fruit of doing—doing the work of God. The fruit of being is called the fruit of the Spirit, and the fruit of doing is the fruit of bringing forth after our kind. This is doing Christian work, doing the things of Christ, winning people to Christ, and producing other Christians.

Every Christian has the responsibility to reproduce himself. With this as a goal, he can look at his life and know whether or not his life is being meaningful and accomplishing what it should. Each of us should be reproducing another Christian. When we leave this world, each of us have the responsibility to reproduce someone like himself who wants to do the work of God and wants to love God as he should.

If we are neglectful in our prayer life, we will be deficient in bearing both the fruit of being and the fruit of doing. The secret of spiritual power and fruitfulness is tarrying much in the secret closet that we spoke of in the previous chapter. Secret closet praying brings many rewards. As I previously asked, "Where is your closet?" Where is that place in your life where you meet with God? Where do you go to pour out your heart to God? Where do you go to worship God? Where do you go to let God speak to you and let God know that you love Him? Where do you go to make your requests known unto God? We all need that one special place—that one place of victory where Jesus is always faithful to meet us. When we find that place and pray in secret, God can reward us openly with the things for which we ask. Let us look at some of the by-products or fruits of a successful prayer life.

First, prayer produces spiritual power. Each of us can remember taking spelling tests in school. When you took a spelling test, if a word was spelled incorrectly, the teacher put one of those red marks by the misspelled word to indicate that the word was spelled incorrectly. If it were spelled correctly, the teacher put a check mark by the word or maybe no mark at all. Prayer is the right way to obtain spiritual power. The person who has the power of the Spirit resting upon him is certainly a person of prayer. When we try to get power in any way other than prayer, there is a spiritual red mark on our attempt.

You cannot know the power of God without spending much time in prayer. If you pray once in a while, you will have no power in your day-to-day life. You will have no power to be a good parent. You will have no power for being a good husband or wife. You will be left to your own devices and strength. The secret of power is getting alone with God and begging for His help and power.

Your age, your place in life, your experience, and even how much you think you know about the Word of God does not matter. The person who has given himself to prayer will have an unusual power, even above those who have been saved longer or have been in church longer. It is not about how long you have been on the church roll. As a church, how much of the power of God do we have? The amount of power God rests on a particular church is not dependent upon the length of time that our church has existed. The power of God comes through our individual prayer lives.

How much of the power of God rests on the decisions that you make every day? How much does the power of God rest on your decisions of life? We are failing today because we go through religious, lethargic exercises and do not spend time with God to get His power. There is no power in music. There is no power in preaching. There is no power in teaching. These are merely tools. Power comes from God. When someone has the power of God, it is evident. I can guarantee you that they have been in the prayer closet for awhile. Prayer leads to spiritual power. If we are going to have spiritual power to see people saved, to run our homes, and to help our friends, children, and loved ones, we are going to have to give ourselves to prayer. We are going to have to determine what it takes to make us successful in prayer.

Secondly, a thriving prayer life leads to success. You may not have what the world deems success, but you are going to have success as God sees it. You will have success in your spiritual walk and in the things that matter. We should seek to become successful, but we have to follow the pathway of prayer to do so. I do not care how much money you have, what your job is, or what your life experience is. I do not consider you a successful person if you do not spend time in prayer with God. If there is no evidence that you have been with God, you are not a success. Most of the answers that we give are things that we have come up with in our minds. We create our own god in our minds. We worship him; we obey him; we listen to him; and the truth of the matter is that is what the average Christian does. As a result, we are not successful and we say, "God is not working." No! There is nothing wrong with God! The problem is with us. If we do not have success, it is not God's fault; it is our fault.

We must follow the pathway of prayer. The prayerful person is a successful person. The prayerful person continues in life even when it seems that everything is against him. When we examine our lives and look at our defeats, we will find that they stem from a lack of prayer. They stem from a lack of spending time with God. While preparing this chapter, I reviewed our church prayer list, and at least half of the people on the prayer list would not be there if they were spiritually right with God. God is going to work in your life, and He is going to deal in your life. The only way to be successful is found in your secret place. Where is that place? It may be your car. It may be a walk in the woods. It may be a special place at your home. It can be anywhere. Where is that place where you have an appointment with the Heavenly Father?

Perhaps you would like someone to sit down and tell you how to handle your children and how to handle your marriage. You have Someone. All you have to do is make an appointment. The problem is that you do not want to have to deal with the sin in your life that is displeasing to Him. You know that it is a futile effort to go to that closet if you were not really in fellowship with Him and ready to accept His direction to success.

Thirdly, prayer brings victory to our lives. When much time is spent in prayer and in touch with God, we build up a spiritual reservoir of power that enables us to stand in the day of trial. Do you know that if you read your Bible, pray faithfully, and spend time with God, you will be sustained. When the evil days come, you will not have to depend on the strength of someone else to rescue you.

Prayer will have built up a reservoir in your life that will enable you to stand. It will help you to endure in two ways. It will help you to endure in defensive warfare and to engage in offensive spiritual warfare. When the attacks of Satan come, if you have prayed, you will have God's defenses at your disposal to protect you. Moreover, you will have the courage, strength, power, and will to mount offenses against Satan. The Bible says that when we resist him, he runs like a coward.

However, you cannot oppose and resist Satan unless you have the power of God to mount an offense against him. Prayer is the only way you can oppose him. Victory always comes to the person who is fortified by the walls of prayer.

Today, your home needs prayer more than ever. You need to fortify your marriage, your children, and your personal life with prayer. You need to fortify everything in your life with prayer. If we are to have revival in this country and in our lives and if God is going to spare us, it will be because we learned to pray. That is why there is no sinful pleasure worthy of the sacrifice of your prayer life.

Fourthly, a prayer life begets holy desires in one's life. Holy desires are normal for a deeply spiritual praying Christian. Holy desires are begotten in the secret place of prayer. You are not going to hear a sermon that will determine whether or not you are going to try to be holy like Christ and live a clean life. You are not going to hear a song that will move you like that. Do you know where you are going to find the holy desire that will not let you go, and will guide you to make the right decisions in life? You will build those desires in the prayer closet. The person who spends time in prayer is naturally going to have holy desires. We go to God in prayer, and He leaves us with desires that are holy. Prayer leads to holy desires, and holy desires lead to prayer. Each enhances and intensifies the other.

The less a person prays, the less he cares for the spiritual, heavenly, and eternal things. God's people need to wake up. If you live a vile, backslidden life of living anyway you want and coming to church whenever you choose, you are not right with God! You do not have holy desires. You know why you do not feel like coming to church? It is because you have not been in your prayer closet.

Isaiah 40:31 says, *But they that wait upon the LORD shall renew their strength; they shall mount up with wings as eagles; they shall run, and not be weary; and they shall walk, and not faint.* What is wrong with our strength? We omit our prayer closet. We do not feel like serving God because we are not praying! The less a person prays, the less he cares for spiritual, heavenly, and eternal things. The more time that he spends in prayer, the more intense his desire will be for God and the things of Heaven.

All holy desires are begotten by the Holy Spirit. He does not beget those desires to tantalize or mock us, but rather to bring those desires to fruition in our lives. You cannot spend time with God in prayer without becoming a changed person in your desires.

I hope you see that every little problem that you have can be answered through prayer. Your spiritual walk, your physical life, and your whole being are dependent upon your prayer life. Prayer begets holy desires. Why do you not feel like serving God? It is because you do not pray. You are a failure in your prayer life. You might say words every day, but the Bible indicates that God does not hear every word we speak in petition to Him. We cannot regard iniquity; we cannot regard sin; we cannot play with these things and expect God to hear our prayers. Where are the days when God's people prayed, wept, and begged God for revival? Where are the days when people could not sing about Jesus without praying and crying? I can tell you what creates these desires. Prayer does! The secret closet does!

Fifthly, prayer opens closed doors and puts life in motion. Prayer is nothing less than talking to God. We do not talk to people if we were not in good fellowship with them. That is why it is important to realize that we must have a prayer life to open the closed doors of life.

We are limited, but God is not limited. He is omnipotent. Prayer is asking God to do that which we are not able to do. He will answer prayers of faith and open doors that no man can shut. That is why you do not have to try to work things out yourself. If God opens a door, there is no man who can shut it or change it. That is why prayer is so important in your life.

Some Christians say, "I believe this is God's will, so I have to push ahead." No, if you really believe that it is God's will, you also believe that no man can alter it. You can wait with patience upon God. Anyone who does not have open doors should search his prayer life to see what is missing. The person who prays much needs to not fear closed doors because the Lord is going to open the doors in his path.

Do you feel like your life is somewhat stuck? Do you feel as if you cannot get traction or get moving? Do you know what is blocking the way? God is not letting you go anywhere because He wants you in the prayer closet. He may let you prosper for a while, but there is going to come a time in your life when you are going to be stuck, and the only way forward is to get to a prayer closet and do business with God. If you do not, you are going to stay where you are until you start sliding backward. That is the reason some say, "I just don't know why I don't get any opportunities. I just don't know why things don't work out for me. I just don't know why things are always going backward." We must realize that the person who lives with God in fellowship and prayer is the one for whom God will provide a way. Throughout our lives as Christians, we need to have a prayer closet.

One of the saddest things in the Christian life is the person who used to have a prayer life and fellowship with God that prays very little now. He used to be greatly used and blessed by the Lord in Christian work, but the blessings have seemed to run dry. What happened? As we get older, if we do not keep progressing, God puts us on a shelf. I personally do not want to be on a shelf. You do not have to go to a place of uselessness. God wants to use all of us in many ways in our lives, but it is up to us. The way you continue being used and stay off the shelf is to stay in the prayer closet. You will not be put on the shelf if you are praying in the closet and keeping busy.

It is also grieving to me to see a Christian who gives up on prayer. No matter how old you become, your children need your prayers; your grandchildren need your prayers; and this nation needs your prayers. The work of God goes forward on the wings of prayer, not on hype and programs. Churches in America are in a mess by adding rock music and worldly programs to their menu in an attempt to attract a crowd. We do not need those things; we need to get in a prayer closet! The prayer closet will make the difference. Sometimes I want to catch hold of people who keep saying, "I want something to do. I want something to do." When you tell them to pray, they act as if they are insulted. The hardest work in the world is prayer. It takes more determination, more faithfulness, more inspiration, and more guts to stay in a prayer closet and pray than it does to fulfill some trivial role.

Prayer opens closed doors. Do you think Paul ever lacked an open door? The Holy Spirit had to restrain him. He had to be restrained from preaching in Asia Minor because God had something even bigger for him. We must look for that opportunity to serve God. We must daily pray for God to use us. Our prayer should be, "God use me. Show me what it is that I can do to enhance Your work and enhance the life of my family."

Paul was current in his prayer life; therefore, it was easy for the Lord to reveal His will to him. Are you up-to-date in your prayer life? We worry about being up-to-date in everything else, but are we current in our prayer life? We must renew our relationship with God daily for God to bless us.

Sixthly, prayer produces a well of joy. Prayer always produces a well of joy. Prayer brings us nigh to God, and it brings God nigh to us. Any person who gets close to God will find there is no joy like the joy of meeting God and the joy that His presence and blessings bring.

Most Christians today are of the "Ho-Hum" variety. They believe that they must jazz up the music a little bit, and church is just not as it used to be. They feel that serving God is not as it used to be. Do you know why? They have not been in the presence of God.

Being defeated in your prayer life results in an unhappy life that does not want to serve God. That Sunday school class where you have been working for so long has become a frustration. You have worked in choir practice for so long that it has become a frustration. People do not stay on the job anymore because they have no joy! If you would meet with Him, you would be in awe. You would be in awe of Who He is. His personality would come into your life, and you could not help but to be happy. If you are sick, you can still be happy. If you are tired, you can still rejoice. Prayer brings joy. It has been said that we all may meet in the same sweet place when we ardently meet at the throne of grace.

David experienced the joy of the presence of the Lord even when he was on the run as an outlaw. He learned from his own experiences. Psalm 16:11 says, *Thou wilt shew me the path of life: in thy presence is fulness of joy; at thy right hand there are pleasures for evermore.* Saul wanted to kill him, but he could not. David said, *in thy presence is fulness of joy.* What did he mean by that? Maybe, to fully understand, we would need to be like David, running in the woods, trying to hide to keep ourselves alive. He said, *in thy presence is fulness of joy; at thy right hand there are pleasures for evermore.* These are not pleasures of this world. If you are saved, you will never be satisfied down here! Our pleasures are at the right hand of God.

Fanny Crosby, that dear blind Gospel hymn writer, expressed the joy of communing with God when she wrote these words:

> O the pure delight of a single hour
> That before Thy throne I spend,
> When I kneel in prayer, and with Thee, my God
> I commune as friend with friend!

I have a Friend that sticketh closer than a brother. I do not need to call a friend on the telephone; I have One waiting on me. I have an audience with Him everyday. My Friend is the wisest One. He never has a discouraging word for me. He never tells me what His problems are. He just listens to my heart.

The joy of His fellowship made Fanny Crosby pen many songs. She cried out for even a closer fellowship, even to be at the Saviour's side as she wrote the following words:

> Draw me nearer, nearer blessed Lord,
> To the cross where Thou hast died.
> Draw me nearer, nearer, nearer blessed Lord,
> To Thy precious, bleeding side.

Oh, my friend! If the crucifixion does not move or stir your soul, you have not been close enough to Him to see that precious bleeding side. We have lost our joy because we do not get close enough to Him to identify with Him. We need to see Who He is and what He did for us! Prayer is what keeps the stream of joy flowing. If the well has become clogged with the cares of this world and the deceitfulness of riches, thank God, it can be dug again. You can open the lines today by confession.

The sin of idolatry is ignoring God. God is affronted and He said, "If you ignore me, I will send my fury against you." If we ignore God, we are prideful. The Bible says that He resisteth the proud; hence, He will resist your prayers. We must dig our spiritual wells again and make up our minds daily to pray, confess, and keep our minds open to the thoughts of joy that are experienced in continual prayer.

Seventhly, prayer tenderizes the spirit and attitude. By remaining in the presence of the Lord, we become more like Him. He is to be the object of our prayers and worship. In prayer, we invite His nature into our lives and take on

His virtues and qualities. Prayer will absorb Christ and His attributes into our minds and hearts. Do you want to be like Jesus? Go to the prayer closet.

Jesus set us an example for us as He called upon His Heavenly Father. The more of Christ that you absorb, the more you will become like Him. He possesses the virtues of compassion, kindness, mercy, grace, a forgiving spirit, and a love which led Him to die for lost souls. We do not have tenderness, love, kindness, or forgiveness because we are not as Christ. The only way to become like Christ is by spending time in the prayer closet.

The person who is deficient in his prayer life will fail to absorb the Spirit of Christ. He then becomes cold and critical, second guessing the Christian life. He will fail to see the virtues of others and will become critical and paranoid. His spirit will become cold, critical, and self-centered. On the other hand, the person who prays will become tender in their spirit and Christ-like in nature, having a forgiving spirit. He will be able to see the good in everyone.

Do you feel as if you are lacking in your spiritual life today? You have to be honest. Do you really have a spiritual life that is filled with prayer? The Bible says that prayer is linked to everything in your life. The prayer closet is linked to your soundness of mind, your soundness of body, and the soundness of everything you do.

Would you like to have spiritual power today? Do you cherish holy desires in your life? Do you want to open doors so that your life is not stuck in neutral? Do you lack joy in your life? Is bitterness permeating your heart? Do you want to have more compassion for lost souls, a more tender spirit, and a greater love for Christ? If you say yes, then where is that place? Where is that place that you go to in order to meet with Him?

The fruits of a prayer life will be evident in your life as you pray and spend time with God. These fruits will help you to deal with life's problems. God tells us how to get all the things that we say we want. If the bumper sticker is true in saying that "Prayer changes things," why is everything still a mess? That statement is in fact true, but people are not praying. They are simply religious. They may even say words and memorized prayers, but only prayer that is genuine will change things.

CHAPTER 4

Things That Should Accompany Prayer

I Kings 8:33-36 states, *When thy people Israel be smitten down before the enemy, because they have sinned against thee, and shall turn again to thee, and confess thy name, and pray, and make supplication unto thee in this house: Then hear thou in heaven, and forgive the sin of thy people Israel, and bring them again unto the land which thou gavest unto their fathers. When heaven is shut up, and there is no rain, because they have sinned against thee; if they pray toward this place, and confess thy name, and turn from their sin, when thou afflictest them: Then hear thou in heaven, and forgive the sin of thy servants, and of thy people Israel, that thou teach them the good way wherein they should walk, and give rain upon thy land, which thou hast given to thy people for an inheritance.*

I believe these verses are very applicable to our day, our country, and our time on this earth. We need showers of blessings again. The Bible very clearly states that healing, forgiving, and victory are to be found in prayer. We are reminded of the things that should accompany prayer in this passage of Scripture. Prayer is not just asking for anything and everything we want, but prayer should be directed toward revealing the glory of God. Furthermore, we cannot live any way that we please and expect to obtain everything we ask from God. There are some commitments that we must make if we are to have effective and powerful prayer lives. These are commitments that not only add faith to our prayers and inspire our prayers, but also help them to go through and touch the throne of grace.

We must remember that, according to the Bible, a great warfare is in process. One of the things that Satan tries to do is to prevent answers to prayer. To get our prayers through, we must live right and have the Holy Spirit's help. The commitments that we make will have great weight in influencing God. It is a good thing to show the Lord the sincerity of our hearts and to tell Him that we need His help.

I want to give you some things that will help your prayers get through to God and influence Him when He hears your prayers. Although these things are often overlooked, they are necessary to help our prayers get through to the heart of God.

The first thing that we can use to aid us in prayers is repentance. This is a word that is greatly misused, and most preachers dare not utter this word because of its misuse. Most churches dare not speak of repentance because it is considered to be a word of great controversy, yet this reasoning should not be so. Repentance is one of the things that is necessary for victory in prayer. Repentance is not a controversial word; it is a Biblical word. At the beginning of this chapter, in verse 33, we read, *When thy people Israel be smitten down before the enemy, because they have sinned against thee, and shall turn again to thee, and confess thy name, and pray.* To "turn again" is repentance. Repentance is an essential element in obtaining salvation. The sinner who repents of his sins will obtain mercy from the Lord. Repentance means "a change of mind, a change of person, a Godly sorrow for sin and failure." We try to make that word mean so many other things, but repentance really has a very simple definition that is necessary for salvation.

Sometimes, we think that repentance is just for lost people; but the truth is that repentance is for all. We think that only the unsaved sinners need to repent, but God's people also need to repent because of their failures. As a matter of fact, we find that the Bible applies repentance almost exclusively to saved people and to nations. God's people must learn to repent because of their failures, shortcomings, and departure from His Word. D. L. Moody profoundly stated that he repented a thousand times more after he was saved than he did in getting saved.

Because we refuse to change our minds about certain things, we are often defeated today. Many times we come before the

Lord; and because of our failures and secret sins, we must have a deep contrition of heart that will move Him to hear our cry. Many of God's people need to learn what it means to repent. In the sense of changing our minds and purposes, we need to repent frequently. What we do not realize is that we are what we think. Do you realize that you may need to change your mind or your mindset? There are good people who cannot bear the thought of changing their ways even if better ways are suggested by the Holy Spirit Himself. Some may have personal or selfish purposes for not changing. To have a Biblical prayer life and to receive answers to your prayers, you must learn to repent. You must learn to change your mind.

None of us have the mind of God; therefore, no one knows what God is doing on any particular issue. I cringe when people say, "I know that this is what God is doing." If I did not discover His purpose in my prayer closet with the Word of God, I would not utter those words. We have to be sure we have the same mind as God. If not, we need to be willing to repent and to change our minds.

You are never too young or too old to repent. Some people think that you cannot teach an old dog new tricks. You can if you let him go hungry. God can let you go hungry. You can hunger for the peace of God and His spiritual blessings just because you have refused to change your mindset.

Most messages that are about repentance are about salvation, but the word *repentance* is repeatedly used in the Bible referencing Christian failure and Christian sin. Repentance is a vital key to answered prayer. You have to repent for your prayers to be answered in the same way that you had to repent to be saved. You cannot effectively pray if you believe that you do not need to change the way that you think. Repentance is one thing that we should bring to our prayer closets to help get our prayers answered.

Secondly, confession is needed. Daniel 9:4-5 says, *And I prayed unto the LORD my God, and made my confession, and said, O Lord, the great and dreadful God, keeping the covenant and mercy to them that love him, and to them that keep his commandments; We have sinned, and have committed iniquity, and have done wickedly, and have rebelled, even by departing from thy precepts and from thy judgments.*

Confession is another action that moves God. The sinner who will confess his sins before the Lord is promised forgiveness. To confess to the Lord means to hide nothing from Him and to unburden all that is not good before Him. Sometimes people pray, but they do not confess. They do not confess because that would require unburdening everything in their hearts that is not good. Many times we play games with God. We come to Him and pray, but we do not talk about the real issues. Oftentimes it is the same when we talk to people. We talk, but avoid the real issues. We can fool people at times, but somehow we believe that we can fool

God in the same way. God knows with whom you are angry or upset. God knows what you are doing when you think no one else does. God knows everything. When we confess, we are to come to unburden everything that is inside. When I pray, I unburden everything.

Daniel said that he unburdened everything within him. He held nothing back. There is nothing that can be so vile or so trivial that it should not be included when we pour our hearts out to God. If we refuse to unburden anything in our lives, it shows that we love the world and sin more than we love God; and He will not answer our prayers. Some people say that there are some things that they just cannot give up. Consequently, they cannot get their prayers answered either.

Repentance and confession—these are two topics that preachers used to preach that are seldom preached anymore. The Bible says that for someone to be saved, he must repent of his sins and confess with his mouth the Lord Jesus. The Bible also says that we have to unburden our souls and confess all that is inside of us if we are to get our prayers answered. The Bible says so much about confession.

The Bible also talks about confession in conjunction with being healed. When a Christian is sick and his sickness is a chastisement from the Lord because of some failure in his life, a confession to the Lord or to others is the condition upon which God will move to answer prayers concerning that affliction. James says, "Is any among you afflicted? Let him pray. Is any merry? Let him sing psalms." Who does it say is to pray? The person who is sick should be the first person to pray. If God is dealing with you about something in your life, go to your prayer closet and unburden your soul about everything. He will acknowledge your prayers. The Holy Spirit will speak to you, and He could take care of your problems right there.

However, if that does not work, you then can ask to be anointed with oil. James continues, *Is any sick among you? let him call for the elders of the church; and let them pray over him, anointing him with oil in the name of the Lord. And the prayer of faith shall save the sick, and the Lord shall raise him up; and if he have committed sins, they shall be forgiven him. Confess your faults one to another, and pray one for another, that ye may be healed. The effectual fervent prayer of a righteous man availeth much.* Remember, you should first pray yourself.

There are faults in all of our lives. Some examples are lack of prayer, lack of reading the Bible, unkindness or lack of wisdom in dealing with others, utterance of hasty or unkind words, fault finding, evil habits, worldliness, and love of worldly things and places. When these and other things that displease God are confessed and forsaken, He will then answer our prayers. Our unkind actions, words spoken out of turn, thoughts of worldliness, love for the world, faultfinding, and bad habits result in prayers that are not answered. Prayers are not getting through to God because we are not following what the Bible so plainly says about prayer.

An honest confession is good for the soul. It will also lift a great load, restore confidence, and let much of Heaven come into our lives. Whenever prayers are not answered, the first thing we should do is examine ourselves and see if we need to make an honest confession.

We are human. When people confess things to other people, they seldom tell everything. That trait carries over into our relationship with God. We do not tell Him everything, but we want answers to our prayers. If we do not tell Him what our attitudes really are, which He already knows, we are not fully confessing. Confess your sins to God, and your needs can be met and prayers answered.

Thirdly, there needs to be self-abasement or humility. Genesis 18:27 says, *And Abraham answered and said, Behold now, I have taken upon me to speak unto the Lord, which am but dust and ashes.* Abraham said that he took it upon himself to speak to God, yet he was but dust and ashes. Abraham is saying, "I cannot believe that I am bold enough to come before God when I am nothing but dust and ashes." That is not usually our attitude when we come before God.

We usualy pray, "Oh God I need this! God, You know I deserve this!" Abraham said that he was nothing but dust and ashes. Humbling ourselves before the Lord moves Him to give His attention to our prayers. Remember, that when we lower ourselves before the Lord, we touch the arm that is beneath us, God's right arm, His everlasting arm. His left arm, which is called His mighty hand, is over us and we are in between His arms. If we touch His mighty hand by rising up in pride, He takes that mighty hand and pushes us down. We must submit ourselves under the mighty hand of God; and, in due season, He will exalt us. He uses one hand to humble us; but when we get to the point where we are down, He lifts us up with His mighty arm. God blesses us by exalting us. When God exalts us, it is edifying to others and gratifying to ourselves.

Every Christian should continuously live in humility if he desires for God to hear and answer his prayers. When we go to our prayer closet, we need to realize that we are nothing but dust and ashes. How dare I walk into the presence of God, have an audience with God, and try to hold out on Him? How dare I walk into the presence of His holiness with that kind of mindset?

Bible-believing Christians know that when we get to Heaven, we will see Jesus and will fall prostrate at His feet. However, we fail to realize that we when enter into His very presence, we enter into real prayer. The Bible teaches that we enter into the very Holy of Holies with God. How dare I enter into His presence with any attitude other than being nothing but ashes and dust and undeserving of His audience? It would be as if I were saying, "I am being somewhat presumptuous, Lord, but here I am."

I cannot come before Him in prayer unless I am willing to repent and confess; therefore, I must come before Him with a clean heart. Our prayers are not being answered because we are insulting God by holding back. We have to confess and humble ourselves by acknowledging that we are nothing.

When you pray, you should not come to God offering any merit or goodness to Him. You must come to God as Abraham did. Study the people in the Bible who had their prayers answered. They were not big shots even though we think that they were. These were people who humbled themselves.

Abraham was called the friend of God. What did Abraham do that was so great? When we study his life, we do not find many great things that he did. However, when he came before God, he came with the attitude that said, "I am just dust and ashes." That is what made him the friend of God.

What made David the man who pleased God? He was a man after God's own heart. He was a man who came in sincere humility before God, and God blessed him for it. There must be humility and a humbling of ourselves.

Fourthly, there must be weeping. When was the last time you prayed and wept? This subject is so uncomfortable. Is it not? It is uncomfortable for me too. I realize how many times my prayers have been a façade. When have we wept? Jeremiah was called the weeping prophet; and in Jeremiah 31:9 he says, *They shall come with weeping, and with supplications will I lead them: I will cause them to walk by the rivers of waters in a straight way, wherein they shall not stumble: for I am a father to Israel, and Ephraim is my firstborn.*

There is a song that my wife sometimes sings: "Tears Are a Language." The Bible teaches us that God bottles our tears. Do you ever wonder why he does? I believe I know why. Our tears are stories. Our tears are talking to God. They are a language.

An infant has no language other than to cry. It does not take a mother long to tell you what type of cry it is. She knows the cry of fear and distress. She knows the cry of loneliness. She knows the cry that comes because the infant wants somebody to be with him. She knows the cry of hunger. How does she know? The baby can only communicate in one way—crying. Tears are a language.

There are different kinds of tears. I am glad the Lord understands all of our tears. Tears should be the expression of an inward, tender feeling that cannot be expressed in words. When in communion with God, there are inward yearnings that we cannot express to the Lord in words, but can only express in tears. There have been many times in my life when I have just sat in the corner of my study with my back against the wall and have done nothing but weep while I was in prayer. I could not say anything. I could only cry.

The Bible says that the Holy Spirit is my Prayer Partner. The Bible says that the Holy Spirit communes with God about what I am saying and what I need. Many times I have shook and cried and wept. Then, in a little while, the peace of God came because God understood my tears. God cannot reject our tears.

We cannot always understand other people's tears, but I am glad God always understands our tears. When we enter into the presence of God as dust and ashes, there ought to be times when we enter and do nothing but to cry and to be overwhelmed that a God like our God would even listen to us. We should be moved at the thought that a God like our God would even let us approach Him or would even let us breathe His name in prayer. That is why prayer is a very personal thing. Prayer in secret is the most powerful prayer because we come into the very presence of God, and it overwhelms us. We enter into prayer with Him, and our suffering becomes His suffering. Our heartache becomes His heartache. Our loneliness becomes His loneliness. Our disappointment becomes His disappointment.

He understands our tears. He understands them so well that He bottles them up and keeps them. In Heaven, if there is a shelf with your name on it, I wonder how many bottles of tears there would be. In a message that I preached on Heaven, I mentioned many things that are going to be in Heaven that we do not expect. I believe this is one of those things. I believe that you will be able to look at your tears one day and realize that God took them all away. The day is coming when He shall wipe all of our tears away. Do you know why He is going to wipe all of our tears away? The reason is that we will no longer have a need for them as we do down here. I will no longer have a need to cry out for peace. I will no longer have a need to cry out for salvation. I will no longer have a need for deliverance from any sin or flaw in my life. I will no longer have to come to Him for others because He will have satisfied everything. Jesus is our all in all, and He is everything we need. When we get to Heaven, we will not need anything; hence, we will not need tears.

You may say, "Well, I don't want to cry. I wouldn't want to live that way. I'm not the crying kind." You want to know why? You are not the *meeting God* kind. You cannot come into His presence as ashes and dust and not fall apart and humble yourself before Him.

A fifth aid to our prayer lives is fasting. *Fasting* is a word that is misunderstood and seldom used. When it is used, it is often used improperly. Acts 13:3 says, *And when they had* *fasted and prayed, and laid their hands on them, they sent them away.* Nehemiah 1:4 says, *And it came to pass, when I heard these words, that I sat down and wept, and mourned certain days, and fasted, and prayed before the God of heaven.*

Fasting is an aid to prayer, but fasting is not what we think it is. Christians often advertise, "I am going to go without food for a week." You are wasting your time. Fasting is supposed to be a secret thing between you and God. Fasting is not going without food and drinking milkshakes instead. Fasting is not just about food. A spiritual fast includes many things. It includes everything in life and everything in this world. It means that we go into a dedicated mode of prayer for a period of days.

Jesus fasted and prayed. What does that mean? He was praying the whole time. Fasting is an aid to your prayer life. It clears your mind, and it puts your focus in one place. It puts the pressure in the right place, and it pleases and honors God when he looks at you and your willingness to give up something. You sacrifice for Him because you want an answer.

If you are fasting, nobody else should know about it. Many times you will hear about people with their public fasts. They are wasting their time because fasting is a personal matter between you and God. The Bible teaches that there are some things in life that you cannot get the victory without prayer and fasting. God blesses the spirit of self-denial. Fasting and praying are two good partners that go together.

Sixthly, watchfulness has to accompany prayer. I Peter 4:7 says, *But the end of all things is at hand: be ye therefore sober, and watch unto prayer.* If there has ever been a time when this verse was needed, it is now because the end of all things is at hand. What does the Bible say about that fact? *Be ye therefore sober.*

People are more childish than ever before. They are living in all the fantasy things of this world. People do not want to grow up and assume responsibility. God says there is one responsibility that we definitely need to assume. The Bible says, be ye therefore sober and do what? *Watch unto prayer.* We are supposed to be serious minded and to pray.

On several occasions, Christ told His disciples to watch and pray. He said, *And what I say unto you I say unto all, Watch.* This term *watch* is important in the New Testament. Generally, this term is used in connection with the end of an age, the second coming of Christ, and prayer. We also learn from the Word of God that sobriety and watchfulness go together. Do you know why you cannot go into the prayer closet and cry and weep? The answer is that you are not sober. You are too busy laughing at the last sinful thing. You are too busy being consumed with letting your flesh have a good time. That is all for which we live. That is all we do. Every day is a party day, when every day needs to be a prayer day. Jesus said to watch!

Care needs to be exercised by every child of God so that he can conduct himself wisely. The temper of our minds should be grave, fixed, and solid. A temperance in the enjoyment of earthly pleasures must be maintained so that the enemy does not hinder us in watching unto prayer. We must be in a sober state that is fit for prayer. That means you have to learn that life is not a fun time all the time. Life is serious. Your responsibilities in life are serious. Your responsibilities as a husband or wife are serious. Your responsibilities as a mother or father are serious. Your responsibilities to your friends are serious. Why? The end is near, and you want God to hear your prayers.

You cannot go into God's presence giggling. We have lost our reverence for God. When I was a child, men in the church would get upset if someone laughed during a baptism or during a song or the sermon, and most definitely, during the invitation and prayer time. Today these events are not a big deal.

Do we not understand before Whom we are coming? We need to be sober, and we need to keep our lives in a state that we are not merely living for ourselves and for fun. The Bible instructs us many times to be sober. Figuratively speaking, when we are in our prayer closet, we need to get that smirk off our face and respect God for Who He is. My father would say, "Boy, you better get that smirk off your face." My Heavenly Father is far greater than my earthly father.

We have to learn that the matter of Christianity is serious. It is not something at which to laugh. It is not to be taken lightly.

Seventhly, real prayer must be accompanied with praise and thanksgiving. In Psalms 66:17, David said, *I cried unto him with my mouth, and he was extolled with my tongue.* In Philippians 4:6, Paul said, *Be careful for nothing; but in every thing by prayer and supplication with thanksgiving let your requests be made known unto God.*We are to praise Him and give thanks to Him. It is a good thing to saturate our prayers with praise and thanks. We must praise Him repeatedly. Prayer does change things. We have to come to Him if we are to be successful. If we have prayed and no answer has come, what do we do? Panic? No, we need to praise Him. Many times have I prayed, "The answer is not here; but God, I am thanking You for it! Praise Your name! I am praising You for being such a wonderful God! I will praise You for taking care of me and my needs!" Praise You that I do not have to worry about a thing!" Start praising God. Thank Him for dying on the cross and for the Blood of Jesus. Thank Him for your food, clothes, and a roof over your head. Thank Him for everything. Praise Him!

Paul was a man of prayer. As we read the writings of Paul, we find that his prayers are full of praise. Think about that. Praying is an emotional thing. We would criticize someone who reads in a public meeting a canned script as a substitute for prayer. A script is no different than many of our prayers. It has as much chance of being answered as our futile exercises.

The greatest combination is prayer and praise. Someone has said that they are as the two wings of a bird. A bird cannot fly with only one wing. Only when both wings are employed does the bird soar into the sky. Similarly, a person who does not sufficiently use the wing of praise in his prayers cannot soar above the trials in his life.

David and Paul set fine examples of men who obtained many answers to prayer and accomplished much for the Lord. They not only prayed much, but they also praised the Lord much. These men were the masters of praise and thanksgiving in the Bible.

We need to practice praising the Lord more. Exalting the Lord will have an uplifting affect on us and our prayer lives. Recall that the Bible says, *Let every thing that hath breath praise the LORD.* If you are breathing, praise the Lord.

I am trying to get you to see that prayer truly is the key to everything. When the Bible says, *Let every thing that hath breath praise the LORD,* God is saying that everything that breathes must pray. Why would you need to praise Him if you do not pray?

We have made such a spectacle of praise and worship. We have trained ourselves and our children to be like little robots and mindless people because we are all following a form. This is not what God intends. The only way we ever discover reality is through prayer. We may be saved and going to Heaven, but we are lacking much spirituality here on this earth.

We need to realize what an awesome honor has been bestowed upon us. When you are talking with God, you are entering a holy place. It is a place where you can meet with God and pour out your heart as you weep and praise God awhile. When you discover that there is nothing of this world left inside to hold on to, God does a work in your life.

Being holy is not keeping a checklist of the Christian life. Being holy is taking on the personality of our Savior in order to become more like Him. That is the only way that we can be more like Him and be holy.

If you are not praying, you cannot have a holy life. There ought to be a place of holy ground in your life. Please find it. This is our great need. Just as the disciples, we must beg God by saying, "Teach us to pray, Master, teach us to pray!" May God do that in our hearts today.

CHAPTER 5

Prayer Defined by God

Hosea 14:1-2 states, *O Israel, return unto the LORD thy God; for thou hast fallen by thine iniquity. Take with you words, and turn to the LORD: say unto him, Take away all iniquity, and receive us graciously: so will we render the calves of our lips.*

I am going to define prayer once again. Prayer is more than just saying words. I have said before that we would criticize people who read their prayers from a piece of paper, but the truth is that many of our prayers are almost as effective. We just pray without the pieces of paper.

If prayer changes things, then why are things not being changed? If prayer gives access to all that God has, then why are Christians living in poverty? Why are we not seeing the blessings of God in our lives today? Whenever we attempt to pray to the Lord, He does not merely listen to the words, but He looks into the hearts of those who are praying. From the Scriptures, we learn that true prayer is a combination of bowing the soul before God, pouring out the heart to God, lifting up the soul unto God, looking unto God in expectancy, seeking the face and the favor of God, calling on His name, and making known our supplication to Him.

Our prayers should be offered intelligently to the Lord. Our desires and thoughts should be expressed in words to Him. Hosea said, "Take with you words." In other words, say what you mean. Know what you need to say, and bring those words to God. The Lord put words into Israel's mouth. He gave them a prayer. He gave them a confession so that they would know what to say. That is the wonderful thing about God. He will give us the words to say; but we, many times in our pride, do not want to say them. Prayer should not just be a wasted time of speaking words that we want to speak to God. We need to find what words God wants to hear so that He can answer our prayers. Our heart's desires must be in tune with His desires. We have to spend time in the Word of God to find out what He wants. Therefore, we need to enter our prayer closets knowing how to pray.

Stated very simply, prayer is asking. God does not have a need that we can fulfill. We ask God for what we need. Prayer is simply talking to God and making a request known unto Him. What a concept to think about—we are talking to God! We are not talking to our neighbor, a friend, or a relative. We are talking to God! We must let this reality take hold of us.

Matthew 7:7-8 says, *Ask, and it shall be given you; seek, and ye shall find; knock, and it shall be opened unto you: For every one that asketh receiveth; and he that seeketh findeth; and to him that knocketh it shall be opened.* God wants us to ask Him, but He wants us to ask Him intelligently. He wants us to ask Him for the desires that are His desires for us and not just our lustful wants. John 14:14 says, *If ye shall ask any thing in my name, I will do it.* John 15:7 states, I*f ye abide in me, and my words abide in you, ye shall ask what ye will, and it shall be done unto you.* Notice that the Bible says, *If…my words abide in you, ye shall ask what ye will.* Ask anything in His will and in His words. Remember, He tells Israel to take these words. We are to take words to God that are words according to His will. Speak them, and He will answer our prayers.

John 16:24 says, *Hitherto have ye asked nothing in my name: ask, and ye shall receive, that your joy may be full.* When you are asking God, there are things that need to be present. There needs to be holy desires. Do you want to be holy, or do you just want your way? Do you have holy desires to be like Jesus and please Him, or do you just want what you want?

There should also be earnest expressions that offer righteous attitudes to the Lord. If you are going to come to the Lord, you need to have the proper attitude. You are asking God, not some man. You are to present yourself before God with feelings of holiness, earnestness, and righteousness. There are several aspects of prayer that need to be considered in its definition. Let us examine each of these and see how it contributes to the definition of prayer.

The first aspect of prayer is that it is bowing the soul and knees before God. Ephesians 3:14 says, *For this cause I bow my knees unto the Father of our Lord Jesus Christ.* Bowing the knees before God is a good act and a good attitude of prayer, faith, and worship. The mere bowing is not prayer; but when it is before God with the object of receiving from Him, it becomes an element of prayer. When I bow my knees before God, I am saying that I do not have what I need.

We have already established that prayer is an act which consists of much more than just saying words. God considers the attitude of our outward being. What is our body language? What is our posture when we come to God? What message are we sending forth when we stand before a holy God? He considers the attitude of the outward being as well as that of the inner man. He considers our feelings, our motives, and the love and desires in our heart. God considers all of these things in answering our prayers. He considers our faith in Him and the words which are in our mouths and in our thoughts when we pray. The act and attitude of getting low before God is taking the right attitude before Him. When our souls bow before Him, He will then stoop down to analyze the desires of our hearts, hear what we have to say, and lift us up again.

When we come to God in prayer, it is a serious matter. We should come in humility as we bow before Him. We do not just walk in, bow before God, and demand from God. You have no right to approach God in that manner. You must come and humbly bow. When you humble yourself, God comes down to you. He not only comes down but also looks into your heart. What does He find there? Does He find hard feelings, bitterness, or lust? He looks into our minds to see what we are thinking. Then the Bible says that He considers our words.

We are supposed to do what is right. When we humbly bow before God, He looks into our hearts and minds as we open them to Him. He hears our words. When we pray these words, we ought to carefully consider what we are saying because of who is going to hear them. We are talking to God! We are talking to Deity! Our words should be thought through and should come from a heart that is moved by the Holy Spirit of God. We must have the Holy Spirit as a Prayer Partner if we are to be successful in our prayer lives.

The second aspect of prayer is that prayer is pouring out the heart to God. I Samuel 1:15 says, *And Hannah answered and said, No, my lord, I am a woman of a sorrowful spirit: I have drunk neither wine nor strong drink, but have poured out my soul before the LORD.* Hannah was seen praying in the temple. She was accused of drunkenness because of the way that she was praying. Of course, we know that was not true.

Psalms 62:8 says, *Trust in him at all times; ye people, pour out your heart before him: God is a refuge for us. Selah.* Pour out your heart before Him. One reason that we fail in our prayer lives is that we come to God and whisper words, but we do not pour out our hearts. Part of praying is pouring out your heart to God. Pouring out the heart is an act of self-emptying.

Often, the reason God cannot work in our lives is that there is no room for Him. Our lives and thoughts are crowded with all kinds of drama, sin, and other things that are not pleasing to God. We are dwelling and feasting on this world, and we have filled our lives with all these things. We have left no room for God to work in our lives.

If we are going to be successful in prayer, we have to have a pouring out of our hearts. The inward feelings and the burdens and desires of the heart of the true saint of God cannot be adequately expressed in words. When these holy desires and feelings are poured out to God, they are cast before Him. Is this done in your prayer life? When we empty ourselves to our wonderful God, He will then fill us. The pouring out of our hearts to the Lord will be accepted by the Lord as a sacrifice to Him. Emptying our hearts makes room for Him. In return, He gives us His benefits, blessings, and favors.

We must learn to honestly pour out our hearts to God. When was the last time that you poured out your heart to

God and just cried, trembled, and shook? You could not even function! Do you remember such a time? He cannot put anything in our hearts until we let something out. That is why it is important to confess our sins every day. We say that we want the blessings of God, but we are too full of ourselves and of sin. We have left no room for God and His blessings to make a difference in our lives.

The third aspect of prayer is that prayer is lifting up the soul unto God. Psalm 25:1 states, *Unto thee, O LORD, do I lift up my soul.* Lamentations 3:41 says, *Let us lift up our heart with our hands unto God in the heavens.* The soul that expresses a spiritual life and a spiritual will can be lifted up to God. This inward longing may express itself in sighs or an inward groaning in prayer. The soul that bows itself before the Lord can then lift up itself unto God, but there must be an utter abandonment unto God.

A full surrender before the Spirit of God will inspire an inward and upward urge which draws the heart to God. This is where we can fail. We cannot lift up our souls because we are cast down. We are cast down because we are not filled with the Holy Spirit. You cannot have an effective prayer life and God cannot use prayer to strengthen and help you because you are not filled with the Holy Spirit! We have to realize that we cannot live lives of sin, selfishness, and earthly lusts and expect God to fill us with His Spirit and hear our prayers. A successful prayer life will not be realized by every

Christian. A successful prayer life can only be found by the Christian who surrenders himself to God. It is through the wings and power of prayer that God does His work.

Some Christians pray hoping that God has heard their prayers. When we pray, we ought to be able to come away shouting the victory and thanking God because we have lifted up our souls to God. When I lift up my soul to Him, I am not discouraged. When I lift up my soul to Him, I am not lacking in confidence. If prayer changes things and God answers prayer, why are we not getting the answers? The reason is that our souls are downcast. We want to tell God how we want things. We want to live the way we want to live, and God wants us to lift our souls up to Him.

The fourth aspect of prayer is looking up to God in expectancy. Psalm 5:3 says, *My voice shalt thou hear in the morning, O LORD; in the morning will I direct my prayer unto thee, and will look up.* Notice that David says that he is going to direct his prayer in the morning; and in the morning, the Lord is going to hear his voice. This is a good thing!

Does God hear your voice in the morning? We go to work and say, "Good morning." Usually, we are insincere. We really want everybody to leave us alone until we have had our coffee! After we have greeted our co-workers, we realize that God has not heard our voice. Before we speak to anybody, God should hear our voice.

Every time I wake in the night, I am going to pray. He is going to hear my voice! Christians do not pray because they do not really believe that God answers prayer. We may have a bumper sticker that says it. We may say it, but we do not really believe it. If we really believed it, then we would constantly be letting Him hear our voice. Ask the average Christian how much time he spends in prayer every day, and take notice of the blank stare that you will receive in response. We should let God hear our voice every day.

Looking up to God with expectancy is an integral part of prayer and faith. It eliminates the "hurry up" spirit in which we pray. After David prayed, he looked up to see the reaction that his prayer had made. Our faces show everything when we look up. What we are trying to do is see the face of God by faith. Do we see approval or disapproval? When David prayed, he expected to see God's approval, which meant to him that the Lord would grant his petition. You know why we do not look up? We do not really believe that He is going to answer our prayers.

If God does not hear your prayers, then it is your fault because you love something else more than Him. You have something in your life that should not be there, and you are not willing to do something that God wants you to do.

David looked to God for an answer to his petition. Prayer is looking up to God in expectation. When I pray, I am not talking to somebody who is limited in what he can do for me as a man. I am not talking to somebody who cannot understand me. I am not talking to somebody who cannot do what I am asking him to do. I am talking to an Almighty God Who cannot only hear me but also knows me. He can see me, and He can provide for me. When you meet the requirements and look up to God in prayer, then you can say, "All right Father, whenever You are ready." He may not answer you at that moment, but you can still look up. You must keep looking for an answer because you know that it is coming.

The fifth aspect of prayer is seeking the face and the favor of God. Earlier, we talked about Abraham saying that he was nothing but ashes and dust, yet he made a petition of God. In Psalm 27:8, David says, *When thou saidst, Seek ye my face; my heart said unto thee, Thy face, LORD, will I seek.* Do you know what prayer is? It is seeking the face of God.

If you want to have a serious, intimate talk with someone, you will want to look into his face. When you seek the face of a person, you are getting his attention. When your eyes are fixed upon his eyes and his eyes meet your eyes, you have obtained recognition.

According to the Bible, prayer is looking directly into the eyes of Jesus. The eyes are the mirror of the soul. The eyes tell all. I am going to look into the eyes of the One Who bled on

Calvary for me. I am going to look into the eyes of the One Who loves me and cares for me like nobody else. When I go to Him in prayer, I am saying, "Jesus, I want to look into Your face. I want to look into Your eyes." That is why you cannot regard iniquity in your heart and be able to commune with the Lord. If a child goes to talk to his parents and he is guilty of something, he cannot look his parents in the eyes. How many times do parents say to their children, "Look me in the eyes." You cannot look someone in the eyes if you are guilty.

Just as a child is guilty of his sin, we cannot look God in the eyes if we do not have a pure mind, heart, and motive. We have to correct that problem before God can give us what we are asking. God wants us to get right.

We intend to seek the face of God and to receive recognition from Him. When we can see His eyes, we know that He hears us. When we look into the eyes of people who we care about and who care about us, there is a recognition, an acknowledgment, a look of approval, and a look that says, "You can have what you want." Establishing that type of contact with God gives us His attention, and our prayers can be answered. Not everything we call prayer gets His attention. He ignores many of the things about which we moan and groan and cry.

We need to come before God with hearts that are clean and minds that are pure. We need to be completely surrendered to Him, loving and wanting to please Him. When we cry out of the depths of our souls, "I want to look into Your face," we have God's attention.

When you pray, realize by faith you are entering into the throne room of God, and the Holy of Holies is there. God is there. Jesus is there. I must look at God's Son, Jesus, Who is my Mediator and my Intercessor. He looks into my eyes, and I must look into His. That is why people who have sin in their lives do not stay long in prayer. It is just as if you were coming to your father, knowing that you are wrong and still wanting something that you know you do not deserve. We have to look into God's eyes.

The sixth aspect of prayer is calling upon the name of the Lord. Genesis 12:8 says, *And he removed from thence unto a mountain on the east of Bethel, and pitched his tent, having Bethel on the west, and Hai on the east: and there he builded an altar unto the LORD, and called upon the name of the LORD.* Psalms 116:4 says, *Then called I upon the name of the LORD; O LORD, I beseech thee, deliver my soul.* Prayer is coming into His presence by faith. This means that you are approaching the throne of grace and bowing there at His feet and calling upon Him. In the Bible, there are several ways to address God. God, Lord, Our Father, Lord God, and Heavenly Father are just a few. This may not seem very important to us, but it reveals our spiritual state.

The sinner cannot come to God. He has no part or claim to the Deity of Christ or to God as Saviour. He must first call upon God, as Saviour, to be saved.

The Christian who always addresses Deity as "God" or "Oh, God" needs to develop a closer, purer, and dearer relationship. When you are close to Him, you do not come to God and say, "Oh great God of Jeroboam and Rehoboam." No, you come to God as "Father" or "Daddy." I come as I would come to my father. That is a relationship of closeness and of fellowship. That is a relationship of being on such terms that we are as one. We share everything, and we get along. What is His is mine and what is mine is His. That is the relationship that we should have.

The seventh aspect of prayer is making supplication to God. Job 8:5 says, *If thou wouldest seek unto God betimes, and make thy supplication to the Almighty.* Daniel 9:3-4 states, *And I set my face unto the Lord God, to seek by prayer and supplications, with fasting, and sackcloth, and ashes: And I prayed unto the LORD my God, and made my confession, and said, O Lord, the great and dreadful God, keeping the covenant and mercy to them that love him, and to them that keep his commandments.* To supplicate is to make a humble entreaty or earnest petition to God. Prayer is the language of wanting and asking. You are not telling God or demanding from God. You are not expecting that God can do anything other than to hear your prayer and to give to you what is best for you. It is the language of wanting and asking.

Prayer may express itself in repetitions. Repetitions, earnest and fervent, are good and are practiced to some extent by all great men of prayer. The Bible does condemn vain repetitions when praying, but repetition in asking for good things is not vain. In Gethsemane, Christ prayed three times for the same thing. Elijah prayed seven times for rain. David, Daniel, and Paul prayed repeatedly for the same things.

Once again, if God answers prayer, why is your life in such a mess? If God answers prayer, why do you have no hope? Why are you confused? If God answers prayer, where is the revival in our lives? Perhaps it is because we need to be repetitious in our prayers.

The truth is that Christians must discover again what it means to pray to a Holy God who will hear us. We should not pray with vain repetitions, but bow ourselves humbly before Him. He will desire to hear our words, and he will let us know that He is willing to let us look into His eyes.

CHAPTER 6

Praying with One Desire

Genesis 18:23-33 states, *And Abraham drew near, and said, Wilt thou also destroy the righteous with the wicked? Peradventure there be fifty righteous within the city: wilt thou also destroy and not spare the place for the fifty righteous that are therein? That be far from thee to do after this manner, to slay the righteous with the wicked: and that the righteous should be as the wicked, that be far from thee: Shall not the Judge of all the earth do right? And the LORD said, If I find in Sodom fifty righteous within the city, then I will spare all the place for their sakes. And Abraham answered and said, Behold now, I have taken upon me to speak unto the Lord, which am but dust and ashes: Peradventure there shall lack five of the fifty righteous: wilt thou destroy all the city for lack of five? And he said, If I find there forty and five, I will not destroy it. And he spake unto him yet again, and said, Peradventure there shall be forty found there. And he said, I will not do it for forty's sake. And he said unto him, Oh let not the Lord be angry, and I will speak: Peradventure there shall thirty be found there. And he said, I will not do it, if I find thirty there. And he said, Behold now, I have taken upon me to speak unto the Lord: Peradventure there shall be twenty found there. And he said, I will not destroy it for twenty's sake. And he said, Oh let not the Lord be angry, and I will speak yet but this once: Peradventure ten shall be found there. And he said, I will not destroy it for ten's sake. And the LORD went his way, as soon as he had left communing with Abraham: and Abraham returned unto his place.*

The aspect of prayer that we are now addressing is praying with one heartfelt desire—asking God for one thing with a great desire. Some think that God is most likely to answer the prayers that are brought before God by the most people. Others believe that He is most likely to answer prayers that ask for the most good or prayers that would benefit the most people. What is the critical factor that leads to answered prayer? It is the most specific and earnest prayer; a prayer that is full of heartfelt desires moves God. It is better to ask for one thing with an earnest desire and to receive it than to ask for many things with little concern for the answer.

We ought to pray for many things and be in a continuous attitude of prayer. That is why we should have a prayer list to help us organize our prayers. However, we need to be careful when we get too many things for which to pray. Sometimes the important prayers in our lives are not answered because we mix them in with a long list of requests. We are saying words, but we are not really communicating with God. There is a natural tendency as the list grows longer to just say the words and not actually pray. Often in that situation, there is no passion or heartfelt desire as we pray. It is good to pray for many things; but when you have a request that needs to be answered urgently from God, you need to beg for a specific answer to that prayer. Communicate to Him that you really want an answer to that one specific thing in your life.

We should pray primarily for the need of the hour. What is the need of the hour in your life? What is the need of your home? What is the need of your church? Bring your need to Him. Ask for what you really need or what He wants to give. Expect a definite, objective answer to that prayer. Our prayers must come from a sincere heart. We must have a sincere desire in order to be positive, pointed, earnest, believing, and fervent in our prayers.

There are very few people who could face God as Abraham did—as dust and ashes. Abraham had the right spirit of heart and mind. He had the right outlook on life. He had the right picture of Who God is, and that is so important in our lives. We have to realize that praying is not just saying words or a ritual. It is a real encounter with God Himself through the work of the Holy Spirit in our lives. All of us have many needs, but all of us also have that one thing that we would give anything for God to answer. We sometimes get so busy in prayer that we overlook that one thing. What is that one thing in your life? Do you have the faith and courage to let God deal with you about it? Let us look at some Biblical illustrations of fervently praying for one thing.

First, Abraham prayed for Lot's deliverance. This entire prayer is centered on one thing—sparing Lot. When the Lord revealed to Abraham that He was about to destroy Sodom, Abraham became concerned about Lot and his family. All of us should be able to think of someone that we care for enough that we become concerned about his destruction. Stop for a moment and think of that person that you know. If you care about someone who is unsaved and on his way to Hell, then your concern should compel you to earnestly pray for them before they die without Christ.

It is hard for me to believe that Lot was a saved man, but the Bible says that he was; therefore, I have to accept that. He was a man who so perverted his life and soul that he was willing to live in that horrible, wicked city. Abraham could not wash his hands of Lot because Lot was his nephew that had lived with him for so many years. Abraham practically reared him and knew that the judgment of God was coming. He had to do something. Are you concerned about loved ones who are backslidden and away from God? Can I remind you that the judgment of God is coming again? God always judges sin. God will not let us get away with sin, individually, or as a nation.

In his prayers, Abraham made six petitions; each petition was very specifically directed at Lot's deliverance. Each succeeding petition to God became more specific than the preceding one. God answered each one in the affirmative.

God did answer Abraham's prayer. The problem was that there were not ten righteous people in Sodom.

The only reason that Lot was able to leave that city alive was by the prayer of Abraham. Ponder that for a moment. Angels brought him forth and set him without the city. Why were they there? They were there because of Abraham's prayer. Unless we get serious about prayer and really learn how to pray, there are people, some related to us, who are going to experience the judgment of God because we did not pray for them. That is a heavy burden to bear; it is a burden that we do not want but too often ignore. The truth is that if revival does not take place in our country, it will be because we do not pray. As we experience more bloodshed and violence in our country, it ought to move us. All the sins and crimes against children in our society today are happening because we are not praying. You can blame Satan, Hollywood, or anyone you want to blame, but the real blame lies at the feet of God's people who have refused to pray for our country and for revival.

Lot was rescued because of prayer. It was the intercession of Abraham that prevented the destruction of Sodom until Lot was out of danger. Judgment still came, but Lot was plucked out and did not have to face it because of Abraham's prayer. He was saved from the judgment. I believe the general opinion would be that Lot was not worth saving, but he was important to somebody who loved him and who had invested in him. Lot was important to Abraham in a special way, and Abraham was important to God because Abraham had said that he was nothing but dust and ashes. He made that petition six consecutive times to God. What happened? Because Abraham prayed and did not let go of that one great thing, God gave it to him.

Secondly, Eliezer, Abraham's servant, prayed for a bride for Isaac. Genesis 24:12-15 says, *And he said, O LORD God of my master Abraham, I pray thee, send me good speed this day, and shew kindness unto my master Abraham. Behold, I stand here by the well of water; and the daughters of the men of the city come out to draw water: And let it come to pass, that the damsel to whom I shall say, Let down thy pitcher, I pray thee, that I may drink; and she shall say, Drink, and I will give thy camels drink also: let the same be she that thou hast appointed for thy servant Isaac; and thereby shall I know that thou hast shewed kindness unto my master. And it came to pass, before he had done speaking, that, behold, Rebekah came out, who was born to Bethuel, son of Milcah, the wife of Nahor, Abraham's brother, with her pitcher upon her shoulder.*

Here is an example of a man praying for one thing for someone else. He wanted to please his master. He was sent to find the bride for the son of his master. Eliezer was specific in the prayer that he offered to God. His one great desire was that he would not make a mistake in choosing the right young lady to become the bride for Isaac. His prayer was definite and specific.

Would it not be wonderful if every one of us found our mate through prayer? Would it not be wonderful if this world had parents who were praying for the future spouse of their children? Instead, it is all too often something that we just let happen. God can make a difference if we pray.

I know who taught Eliezer to pray—Abraham. Eliezer was Abraham's servant. Abraham told him to go get a bride for his son. Eliezer only knew one way to do it. He was just a servant, probably not a well-spoken man. He mimicked his master. He went to God in prayer having one thing on his mind. Eliezer made the request to Rebekah. She proceeded to do exactly what he had stipulated in his prayer. He acknowledged the answer from the Lord and worshipped Him. Knowing that God had answered his prayer, he proceeded to secure her. It is a wonderful thing when you know it is God Who answers your prayers. We let so many things in our lives happen by chance—a chance meeting, a chance proposition—instead of letting God provide us with what we need. People have needs that will not be met unless we go to the Lord for them.

Eliezer is a great example of someone who went to God for someone else and had his prayer answered. God is moved most when we care about and pray for other people. All of us know someone with a great need. What are we doing about it? We can write sympathetic notes or say sympathetic things, but the greatest thing that we can do for anybody with a great need is pray for him. We can hold him up to God in prayer.

Thirdly, Moses prayed for Miriam's healing. Numbers 12:13 states, *And Moses cried unto the LORD, saying, Heal her now, O God, I beseech thee.* Miriam and Aaron had spoken against Moses because the sin of jealousy was in their hearts. The Lord swiftly visited judgment on Miriam, and she became leprous all over. Leprosy did not break out on Aaron. Why? He was God's high priest. Leprosy was a sign of sin. God would not allow leprosy to break out upon him because Aaron had admitted his sin and folly. Aaron spoke to Moses saying, *"Alas, my lord, I beseech thee, lay not the sin upon us, wherein we have done foolishly, and wherein we have sinned."*

I am glad that God hears the cry of a sinner. He hears our cry even when we make a mistake and do something that we should not do. Moses prayed a prayer for Miriam who was afflicted with leprosy. Moses, in his meekness and patience, graciously and instantly prayed to the Lord an earnest, short prayer for Miriam's healing. The Lord healed her instantly.

Miriam was afflicted with leprosy immediately, and she was healed immediately. Why was she healed? It was because of Moses' prayer and concern. He was not offended. His response could have been, "They should not have said that about me. They made me look bad in front of everybody. They have ruined my life. They have ruined my ministry and have embarrassed me." Fortunately for Miriam, Moses immediately prayed for his sister.

Are you not glad God loves even the critics! However, somebody needs to pray for them. People get into trouble, and they need prayer. People make mistakes, and our first reaction is to criticize them. The first thing we want to do is to point them out. The first thing that Moses did was pray, *"Heal her now, O God, I beseech Thee,"* and God did it.

You may know someone whose life is in trouble, and he will not make it unless you pray for him. God puts people in our lives for a reason, even if we just know his name or face. People have needs and make mistakes. If we do not pray for them, they are doomed. That is why it is important that we learn that God will answer a prayer for specific things. In Miriam and Aaron's case, we see prayer for a loved one who has done wrong and is away from God and is therefore being judged by God. However, the judgment of God can be stayed. An individual was saved because of Abraham's love and concern. God stopped judgment upon Miriam because of Moses' prayer. In the illustration with Lot, we saw God's judgment withheld upon a city. We must learn how to pray for specific things.

Fourthly, Samson prayed for supernatural strength. Judges 16:28 says, *And Samson called unto the LORD, and said, O Lord GOD, remember me, I pray thee, and strengthen me, I pray thee,* *only this once, O God, that I may be at once avenged of the Philistines for my two eyes.* This was Sampson's prayer for supernatural strength. This was Sampson's final prayer—his dying prayer. One notable thing about this prayer is its intensity. How wonderful would it be if the last prayer that we prayed in this world would be such an intense prayer to God!

Samson was a man who was shamed by his sin. He said, "I want one more thing, God." His prayer was so intense that it was stronger than his desire for life. He did not care about life. He only cared about his prayer being answered. The prayer was a prayer of one desire. It was not a prayer for a general thing with a desire for a general answer. The prayer was specific. His desire was specific. His objective was specific, and the answer was specific. It brought specific results!

Oh, that we might learn to pray specifically. God wants to hear our words. Our prayers need to be specific. Our prayers need to be intense, asking God to do certain things for us. How intense would your prayer be if it were to save your child? How intense would your prayer be if it were to save your home? The question now is how intense is your prayer when it is for the glory of God? We whine, cry, and blubber because we do not really care what God wants. Like Samson, we need to pray specifically and talk specifically to God. Samson received a specific answer to his prayer, and God can do the same for you.

Fifthly, Hannah prayed for a son. I Samuel 1:27 says, *For this child I prayed; and the LORD hath given me my petition which I asked of him.* Hannah was greatly burdened because of the failure of Eli the high priest and his sons. Since Israel lived in such a low spiritual condition, God was not able to select a leader from the men of Israel. The fact that Hannah was childless made her an object of reproach. She had one supreme desire for a son whom she could dedicate to the Lord to become a leader of Israel. She desired a son who could lead Israel back to God. She went to the temple and prayed with such intensity that Eli thought that she was drunk. She was ridiculed, but she had one desire—a son who could become the leader of Israel.

Hannah prayed earnestly for her one supreme desire and ambition for her life. This was all for which she lived. This desire expressed itself in a prayer of one petition, and the Lord answered her prayer. He gave her a son who became a judge, prophet, reformer, and revivalist for Israel. Israel was given more time and was spared because of one woman who had one supreme desire for which she prayed.

Through Hannah's example, we ought to be convicted about praying for God to use our children. We ought to be concerned about God using our families to bring about revival. If you do not have a child, pray for someone else's child. Sunday school teachers, you have all those children in your spiritual care every week. How much do you pray for them every week? How many times have you called their names out to God? Are you a Sunday school teacher for your sake or theirs? We need to be serious about this. When God puts people in our lives, we ought to be praying for them. We ought to be asking God to meet their needs and to transform them.

Sixthly, Elijah prayed for fire to fall. I Kings 18:36-38 says, *And it came to pass at the time of the offering of the evening sacrifice, that Elijah the prophet came near, and said, LORD God of Abraham, Isaac, and of Israel, let it be known this day that thou art God in Israel, and that I am thy servant, and that I have done all these things at thy word. Hear me, O LORD, hear me, that this people may know that thou art the LORD God, and that thou hast turned their heart back again. Then the fire of the LORD fell, and consumed the burnt sacrifice, and the wood, and the stones, and the dust, and licked up the water that was in the trench.*

As you read his prayer, it is not very flowery but rather right to the point. That is the kind of person Elijah was. He prayed for one thing—for fire to fall on his sacrifice so that all of Israel would know that Jehovah was the true God and that Baal was just a lifeless idol.

There are only sixty-three words in his prayer. That is not a long prayer; but it was a fervent, specific prayer which probably took less than forty seconds to speak. God answered the prayer, and fire fell. Think of that. Elijah spoke sixty-three words, and immediately the fire fell. In less than a minute, Elijah transformed the nation of Israel. In less than a minute, he changed the religious thought of Israel. What a prayer! The people observed that the fire consumed the sacrifice, the stones, and the water. They acknowledged the Lord, falling upon their faces and shouting, "*The LORD, He is the God; the LORD, He is the God*!" One man and forty seconds in prayer changed people from skeptics worshiping Baal to believers in God.

Remember that Elijah had been away for several years. Do you wonder what he was doing during that time? I know what he was doing. He was praying, "Oh God, save my country. Oh God, send revival." We like that forty-second prayer, but we do not like the years of having to walk and pray. We want instant success. You may have to pray for one thing for a long time before the answer to that one prayer comes.

Prayer is agony and work. What is that one specific thing in your life? Are you thinking about it? I would like for each of us to be able to testify, "The Lord, He is God. He did what I needed. He took care of what I needed."

Seventhly, the blind man prayed for sight. Luke 18:38 says, *And he cried, saying, Jesus, thou Son of David, have mercy on me.* Luke 18:41 states, *Saying, What wilt thou that I shall do unto thee? And he said, Lord, that I may receive my sight.* The blind man, Bartimaeus, did not ask for money. He did not ask for better living conditions. He just said, "I want to see!"

You might ask, "Don't you have to say more than that?" We are seeing the prayers of people who were rich and those who were poor, those who had a good vocabulary and those who had little vocabulary, those who had the ability to speak well and one here who just simply cried, "I want to see!" Blind Bartimaeus had one desire, to see. He offered a prayer of petition for his sight. His prayer was a cry, and his cry was a prayer.

When the Lord acknowledged him, he threw away his garment and went to the Lord. He did not want anything to impede or hinder him in coming to Christ. Jesus asked him, "*What wilt thou that I shall do unto thee*?"

Bartimaeus' petition was directive and decisive: "Lord, that I may receive my sight." What a short prayer! One of our problems is that we want everything our way. We are not willing to throw our coats aside. We are not willing to turn aside. We are not willing to put aside all the things in life that are hindering us. This man would have given anything to have his sight. It was his faith that saved him. Jesus passed by. It was an hour of crisis for Bartimaeus, and he recognized it. Is this the hour of crisis for that one thing in your life? Is your back against the wall? Is your problem draining you? This could be your hour of crisis. You must recognize it.

This man was blind; and he encountered hindrances, obstructions, and discouragements. He was with a host of unsympathetic people, but he would not be silenced by them. The more they tried to suppress him, the more insistent he became.

That is usually what stops our prayers, is it not? We encounter pressure, opposition, obstacles, and fear. We say, "I can't get to Him. I just have one voice, and there are so many people that He will never hear me." Bartimaeus encountered his hour of crisis, and he was rewarded because he took advantage of it.

We must make our prayers decisive and earnest because this will move God to give us the desires of our heart and increase our faith. Do not be afraid to pray specific prayers. I know people who are afraid to pray about things. Some of you have things in your life that you would not share with others. You have it shut up inside of you. It is the source of all your fears and discouragement. It is the source of all your failure. Every time you try to stand up, it knocks you down. Why do you not do something about it?

Some of you have a "hopeless" situation that you look at each day and conclude that it cannot change. Your situation can change if you become serious in praying about that one specific thing. Why do you not pray for that one specific thing today with a zeal like no other zeal? Beg God to give it to you, and see what it does for your faith. See what it does for your life. We need to pray for big things again. We need to ask God to give us big things. We need to have testimonies of answered prayers—of recently answered prayers.

What is your big thing? Whatever it is, prayer is the answer. You need to realize that nobody is going to pray for your big thing as you can. Do you know why? People are not going to think that your "big thing" is as important as their "big thing." You are helpless if you are going to depend on other people to pray for you. It is nice if they do, but you need to go to God yourself.

You need to pray in secret so that He can hear you and reward you openly. You must make time to pray. Your prayer should be, "Oh God, I have to have this or die! Oh God, I am nothing but dust and ashes. I am coming into Your presence, Lord, and I know I am not worthy, but God, I have to have it!" What is that thing? I do not want to just sit around and let our country fail. I do not want to just sit around and be useless and worthless. I do not want to live a discouraged life. Is there a burden? Are there tears? Are there desires? Are there secret longings that you tell to God that you do not tell to anybody else? It is time to find that prayer closet. We need to find God and look into His face.

CHAPTER 7

Prerequisites for Answered Prayer

Jeremiah 29:12-14 says, *Then shall ye call upon me, and ye shall go and pray unto me, and I will hearken unto you. And ye shall seek me, and find me, when ye shall search for me with all your heart. And I will be found of you, saith the LORD: and I will turn away your captivity, and I will gather you from all the nations, and from all the places whither I have driven you, saith the LORD; and I will bring you again into the place whence I caused you to be carried away captive.*

The Bible tells us that prayer is the key to our lives and the key to revival. We will never have revival in America without prayer. No spiritual awakening has come from preaching, teaching, singing, or anything other than God's people praying for it. Some of us used to have good prayer lives. Others never had a prayer life. Whatever the case, we all must get our prayer lives in order, and we have to do it God's way.

Sometimes we ask why our prayers are not answered. One reason is that we cannot live without regard to God's laws and expect Him to answer our prayers. If we want what God has promised in His Word, we must do as He has commanded in His Word. We have seen that God resists the proud. Our pride can lead us to adhere to what we want and how we feel rather than adhering to His Word. When this happens, God is not pleased; and He refuses to honor our prayers. We must remember that if we want God to answer our prayers, we have to do our part.

The Lord will keep His Word at any cost. He will do as He has promised, but we often do not want to do our part. We come to God in prayer as if we had done our part and met His conditions, but our hearts are not right. We come to God with bitterness against others and against life. Perhaps we are not trusting Him, or we have no devotional life with Him. When we come with an unprepared heart, we are not going to persuade God. The Lord must be either persuaded or willing to grant our requests. You cannot push or force God to do your will. We have to realize that it is not our viewpoint, but God's that counts. You cannot tell God some story that will convince Him to answer your prayers because God knows who you truly are.

If you want answers to your prayers, you must become concerned about fulfilling your responsibilities and meeting the conditions He has set forth in His Word. It does not matter what you feel or think. God does not hear everybody who says they are praying. He only hears those who meet the conditions that He sets forth in His Word. He can hear your confession of sins and your prayer to Him to be saved. He can hear the heathen who want to be saved but do not know how, and He will send someone to present them with the Gospel. However, God does not hear the prayers of people who willfully ignore Him and then suddenly run to Him as the great escape from their problems. There are several prerequisites for answered prayer.

First, seek God with all of your heart. Notice in Jeremiah 29:12-14 that you find the words *shall* and *will.* The *shall*s are all on man's part, and the *will*s are all on God's part. Man's *shall*s come before God's *will*s. *Then shall ye call upon me, and ye shall go and pray unto me* [and then] *I will hearken unto you. Ye shall seek me, and find me, when ye shall search for me with all your heart* [and then] *I will be found of you, saith the LORD: and I will turn away your captivity, and I will gather you from all the nations, and from all the places whither I have driven you, saith the LORD; and I will bring you again into the place whence I caused you to be carried away captive.* God answers when we do what we are supposed to do. Man *shall* and God *will.* If I do what God wants me to do and obey Him, He will answer my prayers, supply my needs, and give me what I need in my life.

Our part is to call, pray, seek, and search after God with all our hearts. Many people might say that they do that. They really do feel as if they seek after God with all their hearts. However, if they really examine their lives, they will see that they often seek half-heartedly after God. We think that we already know His will for our lives; and believing that we are in His will, we expect Him to answer our prayers. We have to ask ourselves the question, "Have I really been calling upon God?"

We have seen in this study that calling upon God involves emotion, tears, a place to pray, a time to pray, and a call upon Him with all our hearts. We say to our sweethearts, "I love you with all my heart!" God wants us to call upon Him with all our hearts. Have we really been praying and seeking after Him as we would seek after a lost fortune? Have we been seeking after His answer to prayer as if it was the most important and valuable thing in the world? Have we searched for Him with all our hearts? Many people only break out in a religious fervor when something comes into their lives that they do not know how to handle. God knows their motives when they come to Him because He knows and searches our hearts. He weighs our thoughts and analyzes our motives.

He knows when we have met His conditions. When these conditions are met, His *will*s will be released. He will do as He has promised. Jeremiah 33:3 says, *Call unto me, and I will answer thee, and shew thee great and mighty things, which thou knowest not.* How are we going to know those things? When we obey God and our *shalls* become evident to Him, God then says, "I will!"

You may have a need in your life that you might even need to be met. You may say, "I need God to do something for me! I need God to come on the scene for me!" Stop and ask yourself if you are doing what you are supposed to do. Are you personally doing what God wants you to do with your life?

When you come to God, you have to cry from your heart, "I shall! I shall obey You! I shall call! I shall love You! I shall do Your will! I shall do it!" God's reply will be, "When you do that, then I will." God does not *will* until we perform our part. You must seek after Him with all of your heart. When you pray, you cannot seek after God with all of your heart if you have not locked yourself up somewhere where you can pour out your heart to Him. Seek Him with all your heart, and you will find God.

Secondly, waiting on the Lord is a prerequisite for prayer. Psalm 40:1 says, *I waited patiently for the LORD; and he inclined unto me, and heard my cry*. David said, *I waited patiently*. We do not like the word *patiently*, but we see that David waited patiently. After he waited, God inclined unto him. When did God incline? God inclined **after** David waited. Isaiah 40:31 says, *But they that wait upon the LORD shall renew their strength; they shall mount up with wings as eagles; they shall run, and not be weary; and they shall walk, and not faint.* Waiting on the Lord is a condition men must meet to obtain answers to prayer.

The word *wait* implies many things. It eliminates and excludes the hurry-up spirit. We live in a world today where everything is hurried. We are all guilty of it. We are in a hurry when we get into our cars. We are in a hurry when we sit down to eat. Everything we do is in a hurry; and if we pray, we hurry through our prayer time too. The only time we think about slowing down in prayer is when we encounter dire circumstances.

As we run out the door, we say, "Oh Lord, I'm running late this morning, please help me and bless me today. Amen." That is one of the reasons that we do not get answers to prayer. We try to hurry God into answering our prayers. When we do not receive any answers to our prayers, we are not truly praying.

The Bible says, *Be still, and know that I am God.* Be still. That is completely against our hurried way of living. God says, "Be still. Stop. If you want to talk to Me, then stop!" You do not like it when you are trying to talk with someone who is in a hurry. He runs by you and rattles something off that you do not even partially understand. You miss the full expression of his heart and mind. You do not know how he really feels about the subject of your "conversation."

To wait on the Lord means to take time to be holy. Take time to calm the soul, and God will answer in His own timely way. Do you have a special time that you have set aside to be holy and to enter into His presence? Have you let your soul become calm and still? When you come before the Heavenly Father, you are coming into the throne room of grace. You should not enter into His presence in a panic. You have to remember that it is God that you are coming to, and that you are in His very presence. Be still and calm. Give God the time that He wants. We have to practice waiting on God.

Waiting on God also implies that we have met His established conditions. If you have done your part, met with God, and know that you are right in your heart, you should have no problem waiting on Him. You should have full assurance that He is going to answer your prayer because you have done everything that He has asked you to do. You have to meet all the prerequisites. Be still, and wait on the Lord. You should have full confidence that He is going to answer your prayer.

Waiting implies serving God, doing as He bids, and then coming back for more orders. I am to pray. I am to take time to be holy. I am to meet all the prerequisites for prayer. What do I do after that? I just need to wait on God. We think we need our answer now, but God knows when the answer needs to come. We just need to meet all the prerequisites.

Does waiting imply that we just stand around until the answer comes? No. That is why He used the word *wait*. Wait also denotes service, like a waiter. When I have done everything that I can, I ask the Lord, "While I am waiting, what can I do?" There are certain things that we know we can do. We can read our Bible. We can be faithful in praying for others and also be faithful in church attendance. We can go soulwinning. We can do all the things that we know we ought to be doing and then look for anything else that we can do for God. As we wait on Him, we show Him that we have faith and that we completely trust Him to answer our prayers.

God is not going to answer your prayer if you quit serving Him and whine about everything that goes wrong. God wants to answer your prayer, but it must be in His way and His time. We must learn to wait.

Waiting should not wear us out. We will say that we are tired of waiting but we are not really waiting. We are not really trusting God. The Bible says that *they that wait upon the LORD shall renew their strength.* The Bible says that we are not going to faint if we are really waiting on the Lord. We know we are not waiting on God if we faint.

Thirdly, we must ask in faith. Matthew 21:22 says, *And all things, whatsoever ye shall ask in prayer, believing, ye shall receive.* We receive answers to prayer because of our faith. Obedience to God will inspire faith in God. Faith and obedience are inseparable. If you are not obeying God, then you do not have faith in Him. To disobey Him means that you lack faith.

Faith in God cannot coexist with disobedience to God. When obedience is cheerfully rendered to the Lord, faith operates automatically and spontaneously.

Faith is not exercised by straining the intellect but is a restful hope, trust, and repose in God's Word. There is no reason to fret or be frantic. We need to wait and continue serving God. If you are fretting, you are hurting yourself; and you are hurting your opportunities to get your prayers answered.

Fourthly, ask according to God's will. I John 5:14 says, *And this is the confidence that we have in him, that, if we ask any thing according to his will, he heareth us.* Too many people selfishly want what they want, but do not want what the Lord wants them to have. This verse says that *if we ask any thing according to his will, he heareth us.* When people do not base their wants on God's will, they wonder why He does not answer their prayers. God will not answer prayers based on selfish motives. We need to find what the Lord wants us to have. When we find out what He wants us to have, then we can ask for it.

How do we find out what God wants for us? The only way we can know what He desires is by studying our Bibles and observing God's promises. What is the will of God? It is found in the Word of God. Finding the will of God is so easy, but we make it so difficult. The will of God is reading your Bible, praying, and letting the Holy Spirit show you from the Word of God what you are supposed to do. That is the will of God.

The will of God is not something that you feel or think you ought to do. It is something that you have received from the Word of God that you know you have to do. It is done by faith. Doing the will of God increases your faith and your belief in the promises of God. If you do not read your Bible, you are not going to know what God's will is and how you should pray. I will not believe you if you tell me that your prayers are being answered if you are not reading your Bible, praying, and living in accordance with His will. The Word of God is plain and clear concerning His will. If it is His will, He will give it to us. How do I know if it is His will? You will know His will by praying and searching for it in the Word of God.

Fifthly, set your love on God. Psalm 91:14-15 says, *Because he hath set his love upon me, therefore will I deliver him: I will set him on high, because he hath known my name. He shall call upon me, and I will answer him: I will be with him in trouble; I will deliver him, and honour him.*

This passage says, *set his love upon me, therefore will I deliver him.* What does this mean? It means that when you make Him the love of your life, He promises to deliver you. What a wonderful promise this is!

We receive so much for so little. Our job and our part is to set our love upon Him, to know His name, and to call upon His name. He has commanded that we love Him *with all thy heart, and with all thy soul, and with all thy strength, and with all thy mind.* When we do this, something special takes place within us. As a result, we will have a good Christian testimony and will live in close communion with Him. To know His name is to truly know Him. To possess His nature and to call on Him is true prayer. We should want to get so close to Him that we become as one. We should know His nature as He knows us. He knows the purity and motives of our heart. He should know that I love Him, and we should set our love upon Him. He should know that we love Him more than anything.

Set your love upon Him today. How much do you love Him? God commands us to love Him more than any human being—more than we love a husband, wife, child, mother, or father. If we do not love Him this deeply, we are not worthy of Him. We should love Him more than anything in this world—jobs, careers, friends, or anything else that would come between you and God. He does not ask us to give up everything; He just asks us to love Him more than anything. When we love Him more, our zeal for Him ought to be greater than the zeal for our family. Our zeal for Him ought to be greater than our zeal for any job. Our zeal for His fellowship ought to be greater than anything else. When we can come to that point in our life, we are in a position for

God to answer our prayers because we have set our love on Him, and He knows it.

Sixthly, abide in Christ. John 15:7 states, *If ye abide in me, and my words abide in you, ye shall ask what ye will, and it shall be done unto you.* Abiding in Christ means dwelling in Him. The word *dwell* means to be present, remain, endure, stand, tarry with, and continue with. When we have a holy heart and are firm and faithful in our Christian lives, God can do something for us. When the Word of God is abiding in us, it means that we are doing as He has commanded in His Word. When we live by His Word with His Word abiding in us, the promise will come true in our lives. This is a true union with Christ that leads to communion with God and a disunion with the world.

Abiding in Christ means that we are in Him. As in the illustration of the branches and the vine, we draw our strength from Him. The Heavenly Father is the husbandman. He exercises care over the vine, which is Christ, and the branches, which are the believers. He is glorified in answering our prayers.

We need to get as close to God as we can, making Him number one in our lives. We must get consumed with Him—consumed with loving Him and abiding in Him. He gets glory from answering our prayers. He wants to be glorified, and one of the ways that we can glorify Him is by letting

Him answer our prayers. We have to let Him answer our prayers by abiding in Him.

Do you abide in Him? You might say, "Well, I read my Bible," but do you abide in Him? Most of us abide in the world because we are focused on our own feelings and thoughts. We are fixated on things that are not important. Jesus Christ should be the most important thing in our lives. If we are permeated by Him, know His will, and abide in Him, He will answer our prayers.

Seventhly, keep God's commandments. I John 3:22 says, *And whatsoever we ask, we receive of him, because we keep his commandments, and do those things that are pleasing in his sight.* Scripture says that there are two basic conditions that the Christian is to meet: keeping God's commandments and doing things which are pleasing in His sight.

Do you really want your prayers answered? Are you keeping His commandments? Jesus said that keeping His commandments is how we prove that we love Him. Do you know anything that God wants you to do that you are not doing? Has God spoken to you about anything that you are refusing to do?

We are to keep His commandments, and we are to do the things that are pleasing in His sight. He sees everything that we do. He sees to whom we speak. He sees every place we go. He knows all about us. The Bible says that we have to obey Him and please Him in our actions. God is watching you today to see if you are pleasing Him. Are you pleasing Him? We cannot get answers to our prayers if we are not.

The only way to please Him is to obey His commandments. You may think that you are doing things that do not hurt anyone but yourself. That is not true. The Bible says that *none of us liveth to himself, and no man dieth to himself.* You have influence on other lives. It is a sad situation when others are hurt because your prayers cannot be answered. Your prayers cannot be heard by God because you cannot pray for them as you should. God is a jealous God, and He keeps a jealous watch over us. We must learn to obey His laws and do as we should.

As a parent, if your children disobey you, what are you going to say when they ask for some money, or when they ask to borrow the car? You will probably say, "Well, you're not doing what I told you to do. You're not obeying me. Why should I give you what you want?" That is our human reasoning. "How dare they come and ask me for something when they are doing what they are doing!" We do the same thing to God. God has the same outlook, and He is not going to bless us for disobeying Him.

You have to know that you deserve an answer to your prayers because you obey Him. If you are obeying Him, you can live like you deserve it. You can look forward to that answer to prayer.

When a Christian has kept God's commandments, he can go even further. One of the ways that we show Jesus that we love Him is by going beyond. People sometimes brag about things that they do in the Christian life. Well, why do you not do more? Do you get to the point where you feel as if you have done enough? Wow! You must have done everything that Jesus did! When you say that you have done enough, you are saying that you have had enough of your prayers answered and enough of God's blessing and His power in your life.

You cannot separate the living of your Christian life from your prayer life and the answers to your prayers. As God's children, we must keep His commandments, obey Him, and strive to do more. If we serve God and go beyond what is asked of us, the result will be good. God gives more than for which we ask. He says that He can give more than we can even conceive. It is important that we learn that we cannot play a game with God. If we want our prayers answered, we are responsible for doing the right thing with our lives.

If you are not getting your prayers answered, find out why. If you do not have confidence that God will answer your prayers, find out why. God wants to answer your prayers. In this study, we see so many ways to get our prayers answered, but there are also many things that can hinder us. Do not let your stubborn will cause you to miss out on the great and mighty things that God has for you. God is going to welcome us home, but He is also going to say, "There is a lot you missed out on. There were many things I wanted to use you for and many things I wanted to give you, but you never asked me for them." We simply do not ask because we are guilty of not loving Him with all of our heart.

Would it not be wonderful if we went back to the time when God's people really prayed? They prayed America into a revival. They prayed that God would withhold His hand of judgment upon us. Would it not be wonderful to know that you are protecting your children and your loved ones because you pray? You may be defeated in many things, but we do not have to be defeated in prayer. Call unto the Lord, and get yourself into a condition where He can hear you and answer your prayers.

CHAPTER 8

What God Does When We Pray in Secret

Matthew 6:6 says, *But thou, when thou prayest, enter into thy closet, and when thou hast shut thy door, pray to thy Father which is in secret; and thy Father which seeth in secret shall reward thee openly.*

Where is your closet? A prayer closet is not necessarily a literal closet, but it is a place where you should meet alone with God. You should have a regular scheduled time to meet with God in that special place to pray.

Scripture states that the way to receive open rewards to your prayers is to spend time with the Lord in your secret closet. The Christian who fails to pray in secret will fall short in his Christian life in public. Have you been around people who display a Christian spirit? Do you wonder how they obtained it? This attitude is acheived by spending time alone with God. They have a closet.

Many large problems can only be prayed through and settled by spending time alone with God in prayer. There are some things in life that cannot be resolved by just whispering a quick little prayer. These problems require that we come to God, pour out our hearts, and share our emotions with Him. We need to spend time with God. We need to make an appointment with God and meet alone with Him in prayer.

Someone has written that to go one day without spending much time in prayer will be felt by the individual. To go two days will cause changes that others could discern. After three days, the world and sinners will recognize the effect.

We may pray silently in company or while we accomplish our daily responsibilities. We should live in an attitude of prayer, always looking to the Lord for love and guidance, as the Bible teaches. We should always have a prayer on our lips; however, these prayers do not take the place of secret closet prayers. When we pray in our secret closets, we pour out our hearts to God; and He, seeing our hearts and knowing us as we are, grants our petitions. Below are listed some Biblical examples of secret closet prayers alone with God and His response to those prayers.

First, Jacob was alone with God. Genesis 32:24 states, *And Jacob was left alone; and there wrestled a man with him until the breaking of the day.* Here we find Jacob alone with God throughout the night.

The pivotal times in Jacob's life were two nights in his life when he was alone with God. The first was at Bethel. On that night, the God of Abraham and Isaac became the God of Jacob. Until then, Jacob had relied on the God of his mother and father. He had depended on his parents' relationship with God, but God was not a reality to him.

Jacob was a deceiver. We know the story of his taking his brother's birthright by deceiving his father. He then fled from home and the fierce anger of Esau. Until that night away from home, Jacob had never had a real encounter with God. On that night, in an open field with stones for pillows, God met with him and talked to him, and Jacob talked to the Lord. This time prepared him to leave the country on a journey to get his wife and equipped him for the next stage of his life. This all happened because he was alone with God that night.

Many people consider this to have been the night of his conversion. The Bible says that a man met him there. This was Jesus, of course. Jacob saw miraculous things take place there when he was alone with God.

Twenty years later, while returning home to face his brother, not knowing how he would be received, Jacob had his second pivotal encounter with God. The Bible says that Jacob was left alone. Sometimes we think being alone is a bad thing. You should not be alone just to be alone, but it is good to be alone with the Lord. We should never be alone with just ourselves because we will talk ourselves into doing things that we should not do and believing things that we should not believe. However, if we are alone with the Lord, then God can do something in our lives.

This encounter with God was the greatest thing that had happened in Jacob's life. The Lord met him, wrestled with him, subdued him, touched his thigh, and crippled him for the rest of his life. More importantly, God told him that *as a prince hast thou power with God and with men.*

What a change that made in his life! He was no longer Jacob, the deceiver. He was Jacob, the prince. He was able to face his brother and his brother's armed men. Jacob must have been afraid because Esau was coming to meet him with 400 armed men who were probably ready to kill him. It does not sound like he was coming to welcome his brother home. Because of Jacob's meeting and life-changing prayer with God, he had been transformed and could prevail. There was an unseen influence and a mighty spirit that overpowered Esau and his band which brought them under submission and enabled the reconciliation of Jacob and Esau.

Jacob could not have prevailed with God against his brother if he had not spent those two nights alone with God. Both times, his life was changed. The reason we do not have many changed lives today is that there are not people who are willing to find that place alone with God and say, "I must commune with God! I do not want to talk with man! I do not want to talk to any human being! I want to talk to God, and I want what God has for my life!" If we want our lives to be changed, we have to follow Jacob's example.

Secondly, Elijah was alone with God. I Kings 17:2-3 says, *And the word of the LORD came unto him, saying, Get thee hence, and turn thee eastward, and hide thyself by the brook Cherith, that is before Jordan.* Elijah was alone with God much of his life. It takes a lonely life to have power with God

Elijah had just made his first appearance before King Ahab. Ahab was the wicked king of Israel who ruled with his wicked wife, Jezebel. Elijah gave this idolatrous king a very short sermon with a startling message. He said that *there shall not be dew nor rain these years, but according to my word.*

As soon as he delivered his message, Elijah was gone. The Lord told him where to go to hide so that he could not be found. Elijah stayed alone, and it did not rain for three years and six months. For three years and six months, Elijah prayed and met with God. He exhausted himself, begging for God's power and Spirit to be upon him. He was being prepared to appear before the king again.

After all that time without rain, King Ahab had hired people to go out to look for Elijah. He wanted to find that preacher and force him to unloose the rain. King Ahab knew that, without rain, they would die.

When King Ahab could not find Elijah, the prophet suddenly appeared to him. He had just come from that meeting with God for three and a half years. He was then ready to confront the king, the nation, the Baal worshippers, and the false prophets. God was with him in public. The offerings were prepared, and the ditches were dug. The water was there. He was making fun of the false prophets, ridiculing them.

That sounds like a fun thing to do, but he could not have done it without the power of God. What kept him from being run through with a sword by one of those soldiers? It was the power of God! For three years and six months, this man had locked himself up in his prayer closet with God. He got what he needed from God. Elijah came out, appeared, called down the fire of God from Heaven, and victory came.

If we are going to have the Lord with us in public giving us great victories before other men, we must learn to seclude ourselves, get alone with God in prayer, fight the battle in prayer, obtain the victory in prayer, obtain the anointing in prayer, obtain the courage in prayer, and obtain the fortitude in secret prayer. Only then can we find victory and reward in public. We are not going to save America unless we have people who once again say, "I am going to pray! I must have the power of God in my life! I am going to get alone with God until God does something in my life so that He can use me in a special way!" We want public results, but we do not want secret prayer.

Where should we get the power? Today, we want to use gimmicks. That is why everybody wants to have a praise band. It is nothing more than hippie, rock, and Devil stuff in our churches. We do all this crazy stuff because we do not have the power of God. We resort to scheming and deceitfulness because we do not have His power in our lives.

God is waiting. *If my people, which are called by my name, shall humble themselves, and pray!* What if God had 10,000 people in America who would go to their prayer closets just once every week or two and say, "I am going to pray all night!" What would happen? We are just like the children of Israel when they blamed God for not answering their prayers. As Isaiah said, "There is nothing wrong with the Lord." He said, *Behold, the LORD'S hand is not shortened, that it cannot save; neither his ear heavy, that it cannot hear: But your iniquities have separated between you and your God, and your sins have hid his face from you, that he will not hear.* Sin will keep you out of the prayer closet.

You can whisper your little prayers and have your little set times when you mumble words, but if God answers prayer, then why are we in such a mess? Our prayers are not being answered because we do not really pray. We do not put thought into it. We do not put time into it. We do not put effort into it. We do not read our Bibles like we should. Elijah appeared, and the armies could not stop him. The king could not give any orders to stop him because Elijah had spent three and a half years in prayer, listening to God, preparing for victory in revival.

Thirdly, Daniel was alone with God. Daniel 10:2 says, *In those days I Daniel was mourning three full weeks.* I have not met anyone lately who has been mourning for three full weeks unless he was mourning the death of his dog, something that did not work out right, a friend who got mad at him, or something else that went wrong in his life. We have unsaved loved ones and we do not even shed a tear. We do not mourn. We have vile, wicked, sinful people destroying our country and its decency, and nobody gets alone with God to weep. When Nehemiah had been weeping over the city of God, his countenance was so changed that the king had to ask him what was wrong with him. It ought to break our hearts that people are going to Hell and our country is on a downward spiral into judgment. Nobody seems to care.

Daniel 10:8 says, *Therefore I was left alone, and saw this great vision, and there remained no strength in me: for my comeliness was turned in me into corruption, and I retained no strength.* Daniel said he was left alone. If you mourned for three weeks, people would probably get away from you too. He said that he continued in his prayer and mourning until all his physical strength was gone. Closet prayer is not an easy thing because it requires all of our strength and all of our being. He said that he retained no strength. God can do something with us when we run out of our strength. Remember, the Bible teaches that when we are weak, He is strong.

Daniel 6:10 says, *Now when Daniel knew that the writing was signed, he went into his house; and his windows being open in his chamber toward Jerusalem, he kneeled upon his knees three times a day, and prayed, and gave thanks before his God, as he did aforetime.* Those wicked leaders told Daniel that he would go to the lions' den if he prayed to anyone other than the king. Daniel heard the decree and went into his house to the place where he always prayed. He did not go to a place where no one could see him. These people knew where he prayed. They knew that this was how they could get him.

He went to the place where he always prayed. That means that Daniel had a regular place of prayer. Daniel had a closet. He had a place where he could go to give his strength and life to God and consequently, receive from God blessings and answers. He prayed the same kind of prayer he always prayed at the same time that he always prayed. That is why God blessed him and delivered him. He was a man of prayer. He was a man of character. He was a great saint. He was greatly beloved, and, at the same time, he was greatly hated. He was greatly beloved by God and angels and greatly hated by Satan and wicked men.

Heaven took great interest in Daniel and made much over him. Everything seemed to work against him in life, but, like Joseph, he always came out on top. For his entire life, we are led to believe that he prayed much. He was a man of holy desires, courage, visions, principles, and prayer.

Having been influenced by the prophet Jeremiah and the good king Josiah, Daniel prayed even as a young man in Jerusalem. He prayed about his lessons. He prayed about his food. He prayed about Nebuchadnezzar's dream before he was cast into the lions' den. He prayed concerning the prophetic visions he received and the release of the Jews from captivity. He prayed for Babylon, the city in which he lived. The fact that he prayed so much in secret explains why he received so many open rewards. He was elevated to second in power. Why? It was because he prayed. If we pray in secret, we will be rewarded publicly. You can pray your little prayers, which are good to pray sometimes, but if you want public recognition by God, you need to pray in secret. If you know of something that needs to be done, then you have to go to the Lord in your secret closet.

Fourthly, John the Baptist was alone with God. Luke 1:80 states, *And the child grew, and waxed strong in spirit, and was in the deserts till the day of his shewing unto Israel.* When John the Baptist was old enough and strong enough, he went into the desert and nobody saw him again until the one day when he just showed up. That is the way God's prophets are. We see in the Bible. God is that way as well.

John was a unique character. He spent his life in solitude. The Bible tells us that he was a great man of prayer. In Luke 11:1 we find, *And it came to pass, that, as he was praying in a certain place, when he ceased, one of his disciples said unto him, Lord, teach us to pray, as John also taught his disciples.* What a compliment! When the disciples asked Jesus to teach them to pray, they asked Him to teach them as John taught his disciples because they had seen answers to those prayers. They saw God do something, and they wanted to learn how to pray like that.

John taught his followers what he practiced. Being alone gave him time to pray and meditate. It took time for his call to burn into his heart, so that when he made his public appearance, he had a burning message that he delivered in the power and inspiration of the Spirit. When John the Baptist came on the scene and said, *Behold the Lamb of God, which taketh away the sin of the world,* it was more than just a few words spoken by a man. Those words were arrows piercing the hearts of the Jews and others who had gathered there that day. They sparked fires burning in their souls, and anger began to swell up in them. Why? His words were not mere words. They were words anointed by the power of God, and they burned and cut asunder. There was conviction. He delivered in the power and inspiration of the Spirit.

If you want to really be used of God, learn from John that you need to be willing to give yourself to prayer. Where is your secret place? If you teach a Sunday school class, where is your closet? Where is that place that you meet with God alone to lift up your Sunday school class to Him? Where is that place that you go to prepare your heart to ensure that, when you come to teach them, it is more than a wasted hour? Is it more than just a little gathering for you to feel good about yourself because you do something that you like to do? Or, have you literally met with God to the point that it becomes a matter of life and death when you teach that class? There are people in that class who are important to God, and you have to inspire, help, and reach them.

Fifthly, Jesus was alone with God the Father. Matthew 14:23 states, *And when he had sent the multitudes away, he went up into a mountain apart to pray: and when the evening was come, he was there alone.* He was there alone. As a man, Christ knew the value of prayer. When Jesus came into this world, not only was He the Son of God and God in the flesh, but He was also the perfect example to you and me. He prayed as we are to pray, and He communed with the Father through prayer.

He spent forty days being tempted by Satan in the wilderness. The Bible tells us that the result of His being alone was that He returned in the power of the Spirit. It was after He returned in the power of the Spirit that He began His public ministry. We read that Christ went away to pray and to be alone with God.

Being alone with God in prayer and meditation is essential to a powerful life. This can be learned from the example of Jesus and of all great spiritual men. Social contacts are essential; however, spiritual seclusion needs to come first in order to make the social contacts effective. One without the other is not complete. It is not God's fault if a Christian practices spiritual isolationism. Christ did not do so nor should Christians. On the other hand, the Christian should not practice continual social activity and contact without begging God for His power.

If you are going to work with people, you need to have the power of God. So many lives are in a mess because people who give advice do not spend time in their prayer closets. If you do not have that walk with God, do not advise people in areas that could affect and possibly ruin their lives and their children's lives. Many people glibly shoot off at the mouth and say things without spending time alone with God. If we want to work with people, one of the requirements should be that we have a closet where we go to pray for the needs of those people. We need to get alone with God and pray for them. Ask God to help them and do His will in their lives. This is what we are missing today. We wonder why we can not help people. The reason is that we do not have a closet. We do not have a place where we go. We must go to the prayer closet and be alone.

Sixthly, Paul was alone with God. Colossians 1:3 says, *We give thanks to God and the Father of our Lord Jesus Christ, praying always for you.* Paul said he was always praying for them. Most of our time needs to be spent in prayer.

Every day, we need to go to God in prayer. We need to first acknowledge who He is, adore Him, and worship Him. Next, we should mention our daily needs and thank Him for meeting them. Then we must ask Him to forgive us of our sins and trespasses, and the remainder of our prayer time should be spent praying for other people. You should not spend most of your prayer time whining to God. It should be spent praying for others. When you pray for others, you are gaining strength from God. You are emptying yourself, and God's power and Spirit are coming into you. You are getting His strength, knowledge, wisdom, and ability to help people.

Paul was a man given to prayer. We see that throughout the books of Acts and the Epistles. We learn that he prayed much. In his writings, he says much about prayer. The secret of his power and success was that he prayed much in secret.

We do not realize how much time saints who are used of God spend in secret prayer. It is not for us to know. It is a secret between that person and God, but the open rewards are evidence of their time in prayer.

When Paul was first converted, he went into Arabia to live in the desert for a period of time. There God prepared him to become Paul the Apostle. Everywhere he went, he was thrown in jail. What did Paul do? He turned that prison into his prayer closet. As a result, Paul's spirit was never down. He said that we should *Rejoice in the Lord alway: and again I say, Rejoice.* All of his writings were about rejoicing. God so moved on him in his prison prayer closets that he wrote many books of the New Testament, including all of the major epistles. His prison prayer closets were his motivation to pray for people while he was there. When he wrote those Epistles, we know that people were on his mind because he mentions them by name. It was Paul's time spent in "prison prayer closets" that enabled him to defeat the devil. Paul's praying while in prison could be the secret of Paul's greatness.

We sometimes find ourselves in situations where we think we cannot do what we need to do. These are the times when we must go to our prayer closet. We cannot be too old to go into a prayer closet. Some people might have several prayer closets because you cannot remember where they are, but we can not get too old to go into them. We cannot get into any shape where you cannot go into a prayer closet. The greatest work of God is done by those who have a closet where they go to pray. That is what God blesses. That is what God uses. Oh, how we need to be bearing fruit from our prayer closets!

What are your possibilities when alone in the prayer closet with God? In James 5:16, we find that it is important to *Confess your faults one to another, and pray one for another, that ye may be healed. The effectual fervent prayer of a righteous man availeth much*. Do you know why you have not been healed? Can you think of anybody in the Bible who gives us an answer to this question? Think of Job. Job was trying to figure out why all those bad things were happening to him. He had people, like his friends, telling him why. The Bible says that the LORD turned the captivity of Job when he prayed for his friends. Also, the LORD gave Job twice as much as he had before. Do you have unresolved health problems, problems with relationships, or other problems that you cannot get settled because you are ignoring James 5:16? You will not confess your faults. You will not pray. If you will not confess and pray, then God cannot answer your prayer. The Bible says, *The effectual fervent prayer of a righteous man availeth much*. What has been true in the lives of many as a result of much secret prayer can become true in your life.

The enemies of Christ knew that his apostles had been with Him. He had ascended into heaven, so how then could they have been with Him? They had been alone with Him in prayer.

A little time with God in secret prayer will make a big difference in the life of someone. That little secret prayer is the one that you do not tell anybody that you are praying.

Most of us need more secret praying. There are some things that you should pray for that no one else on this earth should know about. There ought to be some things that are such a burden and need for you that they are just between you and God. God has to show Himself to you! You have to find Him and see Him!

We spend so little time in secret prayer and spend so much time with men and material things. We spend so little time in communion with God and too much time with the things of this world. It is hard for a deeply spiritual person to understand someone who does not want to be alone with God. Those who are never alone with God do not accomplish much for the Lord. We should want to be alone with the Lord. The world will not understand us, but how could they understand the sweet time we have in communion with our Saviour? How many times in the Bible did Jesus show up and turn a secret prayer closet into a revival meeting and time of rejoicing! In that closet, you can have faith that He is going to answer your prayers and meet your needs. It is not bad to be alone if you are alone with God!

America has used up all the blessings from the past. God has blessed those grandmothers who used to pray, those mothers who used to pray, and those men of God who used to pray. God has blessed and honored their prayers, but our day will not be spared unless we again have mothers and fathers who pray.

When we want things in our lives, we tend to ask others to pray on our behalf. That is not the way to receive these things. It is time we expose the type of praying that is not of God. When you were a child, you did not go to somebody else's parents to ask for your needs. You went to your own parents. When you want something from God, you need to ask Him for it. You must ask God for yourself.

We ask others to pray for us because we are not willing to do what is necessary. We are not willing to get right with God. We know that He requires pure motives, pure hearts, and pure minds.

People who do not even read their Bibles want God to bless them. That is impossible. We want God to bless us when we cannot even serve Him and be faithful. This is impossible.

When we get into the Bible and find out what God really says about prayer, it is easy to understand why we are in such a mess. Yes, God answers prayers, but we are really not praying. I challenge you to find your closet or spot where God knows that you are going to be. He will be there. He will always be ready to hear what you have to say. He will always respond to you as your loving Heavenly Father.

God wants to do something for you. God has miracles he can work in your life. *Call unto me, and I will answer thee, and shew thee great and mighty things, which thou knowest not.* God has many good things for you, but you cannot get them unless you ask. The byproducts of prayer are those *great and mighty things* that we do not even comprehend.

What if just a few people would reach out to get hold of God? God can do something if you are willing to meet with Him and allow Him to do something with your life. Go out into your backyard or some other place. Talk to God and pour out your soul. Weep, and let Him see the sincerity of your broken heart. Beg Him. He is a good God. He loves you and wants to answer your prayers. Find that closet or that place where God can bless you, and then see the public blessings on your home, your church, and on America. We cannot see those public things unless we meet with Him in secret.

CHAPTER 9

Does God Hear You?

John 11:41 states, *Then they took away the stone from the place where the dead was laid. And Jesus lifted up his eyes, and said, Father, I thank thee that thou hast heard me.* Jesus said, *Father, I thank thee that thou hast heard me.* What a wonderful and exciting thing it is to know that God is listening! We know that He heard Jesus, but the important question is, does He hear you?

I have posed a question from the beginning of this book that, if God answers prayer and so many people are praying, why are we in such a mess? Why are our homes in such a mess? Why are so many lives in such a mess? The answer is simple. Prayers are not being answered because most people are not truly praying. They go through religious exercises that mean absolutely nothing.

We have seen in this study that you must have the right words when you pray, and the only way to get the right words is to spend time in the Word of God. You cannot separate your devotional life from your prayer life. You must have certain things in order. The requirements for answered prayer and needs that we have are given to us in the Word of God.

In the verse referenced, Jesus says, *I thank thee that thou hast heard me.* Can you say that Jesus has heard you during the past week? Has God heard your requests this week? The Christian who wants to be pleasing to God will be greatly concerned that his prayers are heard and answered.

The best prayer book that you can find is the Bible. It should be read and studied with the objective of learning how to get answers to your prayers. If your prayers are not being answered, the Bible can reveal the reasons. If you are concerned about your prayer life and believe that God is not listening, you need to study to find out why. If you do not care, there is something wrong with you. All of us should be concerned about our prayer lives. Let us look at several Biblical reasons for unanswered prayer.

First, pride and self-righteousness hinder prayers. In Job 35:12-13 we find, *There they cry, but none giveth answer, because of the pride of evil men. Surely God will not hear vanity, neither will the Almighty regard it.* One thing that hinders prayers is pride—pride in yourself and your own personal righteousness. *There they cry, but none giveth answer.* They cry, but nobody answers because of pride. He will neither hear nor regard our prayers when we pray with pride and self-righteousness.

In Luke 18:11-14, we read about the prayers of the Pharisee and the Publican. *The Pharisee stood and prayed thus with himself....* Who was he praying to? It is important to notice that it says that he was praying with himself. That is how most people pray. They pray to themselves because in their minds they are God. They will not admit that; but in their minds, they decide what is right and wrong. In their minds, they can decide what they do and do not do. In their minds, they can decide how they live. When they pray, they pray to themselves. The Bible says that the Pharisee *prayed thus with himself, God, I thank thee, that I am not as other men are, extortioners, unjust, adulterers, or even as this publican. I fast twice in the week, I give tithes of all that I possess. And the publican, standing afar off, would not lift up so much as his eyes unto heaven, but smote upon his breast, saying, God be merciful to me a sinner. I tell you, this man went down to his house justified rather than the other: for every one that exalteth himself shall be abased; and he that humbleth himself shall be exalted.*

The self-righteous Pharisee was proud and boastful. He was intellectually and physically all that he needed. He lived a lifestyle based on his own standards. He came to the temple with the pretense of prayer but did not pray to God. He prayed to himself! Read his prayer, keeping in mind that prayer is asking God for something. Take note that he did not ask God for one thing. He had no desire for anything from God, and his prayer was not offered as a petition to Him. Rather than praying, this self-indulgent, vain man made a mockery of prayer. He was praising himself, boasting of his goodness and works, and condemning the publican. He employed the personal pronoun *I* six times. His prayer was negative, so God did not justify him.

The Bible says in James 4:6 that *God resisteth the proud.* If you will not humble yourself in prayer, God says He will resist you because of your pride. If you are filled with pride like the Pharisee, He will be against your prayers and anything you do.

From the Publican's prayer, we learn that humility, the opposite of pride, is a potent factor in getting prayers through to God and getting answers. God can see you as you are. No one can stand before God in pride. You have to humble and abase yourself. Realize that you are entering into His presence in the Holy of Holies. You are entering into the presence of Deity. You are looking into the face of Jesus. Humbly beseech the Lord to hear you. Pride and self-righteousness in your attitude will hinder your prayers.

Secondly, disobeying God's laws hinders prayer. Proverbs 28:9 clearly states, *He that turneth away his ear from hearing the law, even his prayer shall be abomination.* There are some prayers that are an abomination to God. If you look at the word *abomination* in Scripture, you will find that it is a very strong and powerful word. It is a word that God uses to express His feelings of anger. When we are disobeying Him, He says of our prayers, "How dare you not live for Me and ignore My

Word, then offer a prayer to Me?" It is like a child who does not obey his parents and comes to them, expecting them to do special favors for him. God says, "How dare you?"

We speak to God in prayer. He speaks to us through His Word. You cannot have a conversation with God unless you are willing to study His Word because that is how He speaks to you. That is how He will answer you. In His Word, we find the right words to take to Him. God speaks to us through His Word, the Holy Spirit, and His divine providences through His ministering servants.

When we obey God, He will hearken to us. When God's laws are disregarded, He will not regard our prayers; rather, they will be an abomination to him. God justly refuses to hear those who do not heed His laws. When our prayers are not being answered, we must check to see if we are disregarding any of His laws. *To him that knoweth to do good, and doeth it not, to him it is sin.*

You cannot have a prayer life without living in the Word of God. You have to come to the Word of God. You cannot pray unless you read the Bible and find out what God says and what He expects of you. If you are saying, "Well, I know I ought to do this, but...," you cannot get your prayers answered. God will not hear you if you disobey Him. As far as God is concerned, it is an abomination for you to ask for anything. It is an abomination for you to call upon Him, expecting Him to do anything. He says that you must hear and obey His law, or He will ignore your prayers.

We have seen in this study how God bottles the tears from our prayers. He saves our prayers because they are going to be answered. You cannot willfully disobey God and then cry, "Oh God, hear my prayers!" Do you have a loved one who has a need? You cannot pray for him. Do you have someone who is dying? You cannot pray for him. Do you have someone who needs comfort? You cannot pray for him because you have ignored the Word of God! It is not a trivial thing whether or not you are reading and living in the Word of God. We need to obey it.

Thirdly, regarding iniquity in the heart hinders prayer. Psalm 66:18 says, *If I regard iniquity in my heart, the Lord will not hear me.* God hates sin with a hatred far greater than we can understand. Man's hatred is nothing in comparison to God's hatred. On the other hand, He loves righteousness. To be like God, we must hate sin and love righteousness. To regard sin means "to see, look at with favor, respect, or approve of it." God hates it and looks at it with abhorrence. We need to have the same attitude toward sin.

Today, we have people who defend sin. We have people who want to participate in sin. If you possess this attitude, you cannot pray. You cannot talk to God. You cannot make requests of Him. You are on your own and will have no help when you need it because you cannot call on Him. If you do not hate what He hates and love what He loves, you are not like Him. We need to hate what God hates.

If you think that a particular sin is not a big deal, you do not have any answered prayers. I have the Bible on my side. If you do not have a problem with things the Bible declares to be sin, you have a problem. You will not have any answered prayers. You need to learn to hate sin because God hates sin. Hate what He hates. Love what He loves. If you do not, you cannot be like Him. If you cherish something He hates, you have to change before your prayers can be answered because sin will stand between you and God.

Sin will keep your prayers from getting through to God, keep your petitions from His presence and cause them to become null and void. The condition of your heart when you pray is more important than how long you pray or even the words you say.

As we have seen in these studies, the Bible says that when we pray, God comes down low so He can look into our hearts and eyes and know our sincerity and attitude toward sin. When we make requests to Him, He knows what our condition is. We must not regard iniquity in our hearts.

Fourthly, offering unworthy service to God hinders prayer. Malachi 1:7-9 says, *Ye offer polluted bread upon mine altar; and ye say,*

Wherein have we polluted thee? In that ye say, The table of the LORD is contemptible. And if ye offer the blind for sacrifice, is it not evil? and if ye offer the lame and sick, is it not evil? offer it now unto thy governor; will he be pleased with thee, or accept thy person? saith the LORD of hosts. And now, I pray you, beseech God that he will be gracious unto us: this hath been by your means: will he regard your persons? saith the LORD of hosts. Did you know that you can serve God and not have your prayers answered? God demands and is worthy of our best. Why do we think we can give God leftovers? God expects our best and should get our best.

In Old Testament times, all offerings brought to God had to be the best. They had to be without spot or blemish. If they were not the best, He did not accept them. God had rules, and He enforced them. God gave His Best to redeem us. In return, He asks for our best.

In the days of Malachi, people were offering the blind, diseased, and lame to the Lord. They were offering animals they did not want or could not use. They also offered polluted bread to Him. The Lord did not accept their sacrifices because they were an abomination to Him.

Some people offer the Lord leftovers, refuse, and scraps after they have indulged in what they want. Such service or offerings will likewise not be accepted by the Lord. We sometimes name with pride what we did for God. Was it your best? Most people give God the leftovers.

Some of you think that you are doing God a great favor by attending church. You think that God should sit up and take notice when you go to church. You are not giving anything to God by coming to church. You are only obeying His command. A person does not deserve God's attention or blessing when his sacrifice and service is at no cost to him. That does not move God to harken to you. God only values that which is of cost to you.

What is your Christian service to God? God looks down and sees us working for Him. Some of us are doing just enough to say, "We are working for God." Others expend the energy to go the extra mile, which costs them physically, financially, and in other ways. God is pleased with that and is moved to accept their sacrifice, answer their prayers, and give them what they need. Remember, you cannot give something to God that He will not repay.

The widow who gave two mites greatly moved the Lord. A millionaire who gives an offering of $2,000 when he owes $100,000 in tithes does not please the Lord because God always considers what we have left. The widow gave it all to Jesus and had nothing left. How much do you have left?

We spend most of our time, effort, and energy on ourselves and brag that we did this or that for the Lord. God deserves the best. If you are going to serve Him, serve Him with all your might. If you want Him to answer your prayers, give

Him the best that you have. Give God sacrifice and service that are pure and unblemished, and He will answer your prayers.

We have so many people who give God the leftovers. They say, "Here is a little token, God." "I went to church. What else does He want?" "I even tithed. What more could He ask?" He wants you to give yourself. He wants you to give your best. He wants your strength—not your weakness. Give what you have to Him. Let Him use it in the right way.

Fifthly, asking amiss hinders prayer. James 4:3 states, *Ye ask, and receive not, because ye ask amiss, that ye may consume it upon your lusts.* Asking amiss is another reason for unanswered prayer. This can include a number of things such as asking perversely for things that God does not want us to have and that are not good for us. We ask for these things for our own pleasure and to satisfy selfish motives. God wisely considers our prayers; and when they are not for His glory or our good, He does not grant what we are asking.

That is one reason Bible study is so important. How do you know how to ask for the right things? You read the Bible. You live in the Word of God. God speaks to you and impresses your heart through His Word.

God only talks to you through the Bible. He does not talk to you in your sleep. He does not communicate with you by making you feel something. When God talks to you, He will speak to you through His Word. Only by studying the Bible can you know for what to ask, how to live, and how to accomplish God's will. When you ask amiss, God says that He will not answer those prayers.

Sixthly, praying with a selfish motive hinders prayer. Again from James 4:3 we find, *...that ye may consume it upon your lusts.* Lust is defined as "an unlawful love and over-desire, a sinful desire." If people could receive the gratification of lustful desires from God, there is no doubt that many of us would pray to be millionaires. If we could get anything we wanted, you know what you would say. "God, I will use it for your glory. God, I will use it to be a blessing to others." God will not answer prayers aimed at satisfying our lusts. We could ask to be famous, beautiful, or popular. We might ask to live long without becoming old, escape death, excel over others in our endeavors, become highly gifted, become champions, and many other things. These things could be detrimental to us and detract from God's glory.

God will not answer prayers that ask Him to satisfy your lusts. Prayer is praising God, thanking Him for what He does for you, asking bread for yourself and others, and asking that other people's needs be met.

Seventhly, wavering at God's promises hinders prayer. James 1:6,7 says, *But let him ask in faith, nothing wavering. For he* *that wavereth is like a wave of the sea driven with the wind and tossed. For let not that man think that he shall receive any thing of the Lord.* The person who is steady and faithful will be honored by God in his prayer life.

In order to be steady, we must have faith. Where do we get this faith? *So then faith cometh by hearing, and hearing by the word of God.* In this study, I hope you have come to see that prayer is the key to the Christian life. It is the whole key to life. The faith we need to pray and the words we use come from God Himself in the Bible. He loves us so much that He gave us the Book telling us how to pray.

The person who allows doubt to control him will be hindered with unbelief. Doubts are like the wind and waves on the sea. Wavering in faith can be likened unto a ship being tossed by the wind and waves. Living by faith is to be lifted up, and doubting is to be cast down. Think of the person who fluctuates between faith and doubt. At one moment, his mind is set toward Heaven as he lives in the glories, intent on entering Heaven, desirous of securing immortality, and expressive of his determination to be faithful to the Lord even unto death. Then, he sinks into doubt and despair, seeking to please the body as he chases worldly enjoyments and pleasures.

Fluctuating between the two states can be likened unto riding the waves of the sea as they rise and fall. This kind of life is never satisfactory. It may satisfy self and the flesh, but it will hinder our prayer lives.

An eye that is single to the glory of God, a heart that is fixed, a mind that has a single interest in the Heavenly, spiritual, and eternal things, and a face set like a flint will be honored by God and move Him to answer prayer. God will not bless you if you are an up-and-down person. If one day you read your Bible and live for Him, and the next day you live for the attractions of the world, many of your prayers will not be answered because of wavering. Of course, God will forgive you. He will let you start over. However, only in Heaven will you know what you have missed because of hindered prayers.

Eighthly, husbands and wives not having the right relationship hinders prayers. I Peter 3:1-7 reads, *Likewise, ye wives, be in subjection to your own husbands; that, if any obey not the word, they also may without the word be won by the conversation of the wives; While they behold your chaste conversation coupled with fear. Whose adorning let it not be that outward adorning of plaiting the hair, and of wearing of gold, or of putting on of apparel; But let it be the hidden man of the heart, in that which is not corruptible, even the ornament of a meek and quiet spirit, which is in the sight of God of great price. For after this manner in the old time the holy women also, who trusted in God, adorned themselves, being in subjection unto their own husbands: Even as Sara obeyed Abraham, calling him lord: whose daughters ye are, as long as ye do well, and are not afraid with* *any amazement. Likewise, ye husbands, dwell with them according to knowledge, giving honour unto the wife, as unto the weaker vessel, and as being heirs together of the grace of life; that your prayers be not hindered.*

Can we tear this out of the Bible? No, we cannot. It boils down to the fact that your being angry or harboring ill will toward anybody will keep God from answering your prayers.

Here, God is specifically addressing husbands and wives. A couple may say, "Well, we just have a little bit of trouble in the house." Resolve it in a hurry because the Bible says your prayers are hindered by your relationship not being right. This is not uncommon. Husbands and wives do not speak with each other. They get angry, fight, and fuss. They continue living in this state, never correcting things at home and never doing the right thing. God says that when you are living like this, your prayers will be hindered. Yelling and screaming at home can cost you your prayer life. Mistreating each other can cost you your prayer life. It is not worth it.

How can you pray for your children? How can you pray for your home? You cannot pray for anything if you are not right with each other. You have to work it out. You have to go to each other and talk about it. If you are not heeding this admonition, your prayers will not be answered. If you follow the Word of God, God will bless you and answer your prayers.

A woman might use the excuse that her husband will not get right, but she can get right. A man may use the excuse that his wife will not get right, but he could get right. It is strange today how we think that somebody else's sin justifies our own. Somebody else is not right with God, and we use that as an excuse for our sin. No! In the Bible, God instructs us for correct behavior in every relationship. If we do not follow His guidance, our prayers will not be answered.

I am excited as I read of Jesus saying, *Father, I thank thee that thou hast heard me.* When we pray, we ought to be able to say the same thing. If we know that He hears us, we know the answer is coming. Have I done all I can? Have I confessed my sins? Have I gotten right with God? Do I have my heart right? Have I humbled myself? Have I had a burdened, heavy heart that sometimes even brings me to tears? Do I pour out my heart to God?

We make fun of people who pray to statues. I have been to great cathedrals and watched people crawl around on the floor, crying, paying money, lighting candles, and praying to statues. We feel sorry for them. We ask God to bless them and help them to know the truth. They are not getting through. They are not praying. There is nothing about their prayer that is proper or Scriptural. It is done out of ignorance. However, our prayers have no more chance of getting through if we do not follow the Biblical pattern of prayer. We might as well light a candle ourselves. It will not work.

Consider a person who is a Buddhist that worships and prays to a statue. We talk about how he is so dumb and crazy. He thinks he will have his prayers answered, and we know that he will not. It is the same for us when we ignore what God says, do what we think is right, follow our own lusts, follow our own minds, and pray to ourselves. We wonder why things are like they are!

If God answers prayer, why is your life like it is? If God answers prayer, why is this world like it is? The answer is that we have the responsibility to pray, and we are not really praying. If we love America, we must pray for her. If we love our children, we must pray for them. If we love our families, we must pray. If we want to please God, serve Him, and face Him unashamed, we have to pray. We cannot pray to ourselves, "Oh God, I am not like Brother So-and-so. You know I do the best I can." That is not prayer. You may say, "Well, I do the best I can." That is not prayer. None of us do the best we can. We do what we say is the best we can. If we were to yield to the Holy Spirit of God, we could do far more than we do.

It is time for us to be able to say with confidence, "Lord, I thank You that You heard me." That is the way we ought to leave our prayer closets. That is the way we ought to leave our time with God. That is the way we ought to leave when we have taken time to be holy with Him. We ought to leave saying, "Lord, thank You that You heard me. Thanks for the audience. Thanks for this time. Thanks for hearing what I had to say."

If you cannot say that, it is not God's fault. It is your fault. It is time to examine your heart. Do not pretend to have a godly prayer life. Let us pray down the blessing of God on our lives, our families, and our nation.

Christian, if you know you are not living right and know that things in your life are not right, it is costing you something, whether you realize it or not. You will not know what it has cost you until you get to Heaven, stand at the Judgment Seat of Christ, and see all the missed opportunities. You will see all the people who suffered. You will recognize the people who were hurt because you did not give yourself to the Lord wholly so that He could use you.

Part of His using you is answering your prayers. He bottles up your tears. When we get to Heaven and stand at the Judgment Seat of Christ, I believe there is going to be a record of all our prayers. Here are all your prayers. Here are all your tears. Here are all your sacrifices. God pays dividends, but He doesn't give away dividends. They have to be earned.

When you say, "I am praying for you," are you lying? If you cannot say, "Father, I am so glad you heard my prayers," you need to get to the point where you can say that with confidence. Would it not be wonderful to go to bed at night, knowing that the Lord heard you and everything is going to be okay? Would it not be nice to say, "The Lord heard me!"

That is why some people have more confidence than others. They can say, "Thank You, Father, for hearing me," and they know that He heard them. Let God speak to your heart. Let Him change your situations and life through answered prayers so that He gets the glory.

CHAPTER 10

Losses Suffered from a Lack of Prayer

James 4:1-2 says, *From whence come wars and fightings among you? come they not hence, even of your lusts that war in your members? Ye lust, and have not: ye kill, and desire to have, and cannot obtain: ye fight and war, yet ye have not, because ye ask not.* In this chapter, we are going to focus on *...ye have not, because ye ask not.* In this Scripture, James is addressing Christians who have desires that they cannot obtain.

People are trying to receive the things they desire from God. In Jeremiah 33:3, God makes us an important promise: *Call unto me, and I will answer thee, and shew thee great and mighty things, which thou knowest not.*

There are many things that God has for us, and the only way that we can get them is by asking Him for them. When we do not ask, we do not receive. It is going to be a shameful thing when we face the Lord one day and see all that we did not receive because we did not ask.

James writes, *ye have not because ye ask not.* That is not a difficult statement to understand. You simply will not receive something if you do not ask for it. Many people do not receive answers to prayers simply because they do not have any prayers to be answered. You must pray if you want answered prayers.

We have seen in this study that we, as Christians, often go through little rituals. We think that we have prayed when we have not really prayed. If you would ask the average person if God answers his prayers, he will say, "Yes, God answers my prayers. Of course, I do not go to church faithfully, and I never read my Bible, I have some things in my life that I know are not right." I have news for you! God does not answer your prayers! God says that if you regard iniquity in your heart, He will not hear you.

We criticize the Catholics for their rosary, but we have our "Baptist rosaries" too. We have these spiritual formalities that we do daily, but we do not get real with God and let Him do anything in our hearts. Many times, what we call a prayer is not really a prayer.

There are things that we do not have because we have not really asked for them. A lack of prayer is the greatest problem in a Christian's life. Only when we get to Heaven will we become fully aware of the defeats and great losses of power and opportunities that resulted from our lack of prayer. In other words, we do not understand how much damage we are doing by not having victorious prayer lives. When we get to Heaven, we will be able to see what God has wrought through the prayers and faith of devout Christians. Men like Moses, Samuel, Elijah, Daniel, and Paul have prominent places in the Bible because they were men of prayer and faith. Whatever you receive at the Judgment Seat of Christ will be because of your prayer and your faith. The successes of your Christian life and the amount of God's blessings are a direct result of your prayer life. You cannot have a successful Christian life without the anointing of God that comes through time spent in prayer.

Looking back at the last chapter, ask yourself, "Does God hear me?" If God answers prayer, then why are we in such a mess? Why are our homes in such a mess? Why are our lives in such a mess? It is because we are not really praying. We must learn to pray. We must say, just as the disciples said to Jesus, *teach us to pray*. Let us look at several losses we experience when we are not serious about the matter of prayer.

First: The Loss of Spiritual Power. Spiritual power comes through prayer, faith, and constant contact with God. You cannot get power from God and become like Him without spending time with Him. Why should God entrust us with Divine power when we have no desire to linger in His presence?

There is a reason that spiritual power rests on certain Christians and certain men of God. That reason is prayer. You can be sure that if somebody has power with God, he spends time in prayer. You do not get power from God by having some *experience*, getting a *tingling*, or coming up with some *secret formula*. The only way to get power from God is to spend time in His presence. Let Him give His power to you.

The Christian worker who has no power is the one who spends no time with God. Many churches and Christian workers are powerless because they have prayerless lives. The best Christian is the one who spends the most time with God. The one who has the most power is the one who spends the most time in His presence. It is a sad fact of the Christian ministry that there are men who were powerful prayer warriors in the past; but now they are prayerless and powerless. Sadly, many preachers had more success as young men than they do now as older men. The reason for this is that they realized at a young age that they could not do it all. Realizing that they had to depend on God, they spent hours in prayer, studied, and meditated as young men. They begged God for His power, anointing, and understanding. They had power and success because they spent time with God and let Him work through them.

Older Christians and preachers tend to cool off and start relying on their experience. They rely on what they know and what they have learned in the past. They are not spending the time that they used to spend in the presence of God. They do not realize that they need Him more now than they did when they were young. They need His presence and His power in their lives.

Look at your life today. Do you have power with God? Is there something real in your heart and soul? When you pray, do you get answers from God? Do you have His strength? Do you have the prayer-inspired confidence to do God's work, or are you afraid to step out in faith? Spending time in prayer, you can get the power of the Holy Spirit in your life and allow God to work through you.

Do you want to be a singer with power? Then, be a singer who prays. Do you want to be a teacher with power? Then be a teacher who prays. Do you want to be a soul winner with power? Be a soul winner who prays. Too much of God's work is being done today without spending time in the closet where we can receive the power that we need from God. Therefore, we suffer the loss of spiritual power.

Secondly: The Loss of Victory. There is always danger after we experience a great victory. We think the battle is over and that we can coast through life using the momentum we gained in the victory. We are not on guard for dangers; we relax and give up praying.

When should we pray with urgency? Every day! When should we pray with fervor? Every day! When should we pray as if the whole world depends on our prayer? Every day! We lose that urgency, and we lose our victory. We cannot afford to coast.

Peter failed to pray even after Christ commanded him three times to do so. Jesus scolded Peter, *What, could ye not watch with me one hour?* Peter could not, but he had all the talk. He had just told Jesus, *Though I should die with thee, yet will I not deny thee.* You can have all the good intentions in the world; but if you do not spend time with God in prayer getting the power you need, you cannot live up to your intentions. The result of Peter's failure to pray was that he lacked courage and spiritual power when the conflict came. A few hours passed, and the mob came for Jesus. Peter was confronted; and he failed, resorting to carnal fighting as he cut off the servant's ear. When we do not have God's power, we act in the flesh. You cannot fight the Lord's battles with a sword. You need to fight with prayer.

Peter then denied the Lord three times. Have you considered why? Did he do it because he was an evil man? Did he do it because he was a bad person? Did he do it because of some unknown sin in his life? No! He did it because he was sleeping when he should have been praying with the Saviour. He had not prayed! When you do not pray, all you have to depend upon is the power of the flesh. You cannot lay up a reserve of God's power.

Every day, we need to go to our prayer closets to seek the power of God. Remember, when we pray, we come into the very presence of God Himself. We enter into the Holy of Holies with God. There He is, high and lifted up! We are in His presence! That is where we get His power. When you spend time with God, you obtain His power and strength; but you can lose that power if you do not maintain a victorious prayer life.

Third: The Loss of Holy Desires. When we fail in our prayer lives, we become indifferent, lose our spiritual fervor, and diminish our desire and burden for prayer. Holy desires only come from the Lord. They do not come from us because we are carnal, our minds are carnal, and we are not holy. Every holy desire we get from the Lord must be cherished, fostered, and nurtured. When the Lord brings a holy desire to a child of God, it is not to mock him because He cannot fulfill it. God wants your desires to be for the things that He has planned for you. He gives you a desire because He wants to give you the object of that desire.

You may think that you cannot do what He is asking or may think that it is too hard for you. You may think you are not able to attain the goal He has set. If you truly want to obtain the goal enough, you can. However, the only way that you will want it enough is by going to Him in prayer and depending on His strength. Through prayer, that desire will grow; and in faith, you can realize it.

God will bring that desire to fruition; but, just as soil is prepared to receive a seed, your heart needs to be prepared for holy desires. When a desire has been planted in the heart, it needs to be guarded and cultivated like a tender plant which, in due time, will yield an increase and bear fruit. Keep praying for that desire in your heart.

God says that He will give us whatever we desire. We may think that means a new car, a new house, and all those temporal things. What it really means is that, in your spiritual walk with God, He will place desires into your heart. It may be to teach, to preach, to be a missionary, to give a certain amount of money, to do something for someone else, or to do something for your mate. God may even put a desire into your heart to do something for someone else's child or for another family. If God puts a desire in your heart, do not pass it off and say, "Well, I could never do that." Take it to God and pray. As you begin to pray, the desire will begin to grow; and, as you keep on praying, your desire will continue to become greater. After a while, God will bring to pass what you have desired.

Some Christians act as if they do not believe the Bible. They are so weak in their faith, courage, and character that they cannot receive what God has for them. When Christians do not spend time in their prayer closets, the holy desires that God gives them will soon wither and die. These desires never mature and come to fruition.

I believe at the Judgment Seat of Christ we will be shown what could have been. We will see what we missed out on because we did not pray. You are going to say, "I used to want to do that." Jesus will reply, "You could have done it. My will was for you to accomplish it, but you quit praying. You quit believing. You quit wanting to be used that way." You can lose your holy desires.

I look at people who have ceased to have a holy desire to do things for God. Today, they are cold and dead. They have no desire for the things of God or for the work of God. Do you know what that tells me? It tells me that they have ceased to enter into His presence. You cannot enter into His presence without a burning desire to do something for God. When you enter into His presence, He will give you holy desires; but you will lose them when you do not pray. There are people who used to be so faithful, but now they are not. They lost their desire because they have no walk or fellowship with God. If they did, they would have a desire. You cannot separate the fellowship from the desire.

Fourth: The Loss of Success. Nothing is sadder in the Christian life than the Christian who is living below his privilege. The Bible says of us, *Wherefore thou art no more a servant, but a son; and if a son, then an heir of God through Christ.* We are the sons of God and joint heirs with Christ! I have privilege! I have access! I have things that are available to me that are not available to people outside the family of

God. Many Christians live below their privilege, but with that privilege comes responsibility. Think of the implication. It is hard to comprehend; but when you fail to fulfill your responsibilities because of your deficient prayer life, many things will be forever left undone!

To have been used by the Lord and then set aside on the shelf because of a short-coming in your prayer life is a sad spiritual tragedy. When we, as Christians, fail to accomplish what God would have us do through our prayers, others will fail to hear the Gospel, see the Spiritual Light, or have their needs met. Samuel said, *God forbid that I should sin against the LORD in ceasing to pray for you.* If I neglect to pray and my prayers could have saved someone or kept him on the straight and narrow, I commit a spiritual crime. I will have to answer to God, not only for not praying, but also for the undone work that God had intended for that other person. We treat this so glibly. We ought to always be mindful of how much we are praying for others. We need to be praying for them because they have a work that needs to be done.

There are souls that hang in the balance! Do we really believe in Hell? Do we really believe that people who are not saved will go there? Do we really believe all that we say we believe? If we do, we must pray!

Do not suffer loss of success because you do not pray. Do not live below your privilege today. God has work to be done in this world, and we are supposed to pray and do all we can to see it done.

Fifth: The Loss of Holy Joy. Many people wonder why they do not have the same joy as their Christian friends. You do not need to go very far to find the reason. A prayerless Christian is a joyless Christian. You cannot laugh at the things of the world if you have the joy of the Lord in your heart. The joy of the Lord motivates, comforts, and inspires you. The only way to get joy is by spending time with God in your prayer closet. If you do not pray much and are honest, you will confess that you have little joy. If you were to pray more, you would have more joy.

Can you imagine anyone returning from a meeting with God in the Holy of Holies saying, "I'm in a bad mood. I don't know what the big deal is. I don't know why everybody is so happy"? You may tell me that you have been praying, but it is obvious that you have not really been with the Lord if you have an attitude like that!

When you spend time with God in real prayer, you will receive some joy in your heart and soul. It does not matter how many enemies, burdens, and heartaches that you have, you can come out of your prayer closet singing, "I've got the joy, joy, joy, joy down in my heart." Just as the song says, you can tell the devil to go sit on a tack. You can be excited about what God is doing in your life.

How could we be awed by God's presence, His Son, and the Blood, and still wish that our lives were better? How could we be unhappy or allow earthly problems to bother us? If you have that attitude, you do not really pray and enter the presence of God. Maybe you went through your "Baptist rosary" or through whatever you call your little exercise. If you actually go into the presence of God and know to whom you are talking, it will do something for you. It will transform everything about you.

You may say, "Well, you don't know how big my problems are." When you are in His presence, you are in the presence of the One Who will make all things right one day. You are in the presence of the One Who says that He is going to wipe away all tears one day. You should come out of the prayer closet saying, "I know that everything is going to be all right because I have been in the presence of God." A defeated attitude stems from a lack of prayer.

Sixth: The Loss of Open Doors. I look at some people who seem to have doors repeatedly opened for them. God uses people who have active prayer lives. If God wants something done, He will call upon those who spend much time talking to and communicating with Him. Others may wonder why God does not seek after them for His work. They need to check their prayer lives to see if they are missing opportunities to serve because they do not pray. We can lose our opportunity to have victorious lives of service because we do not pray.

Seventh: The Loss of a Compassionate Spirit. People who fail in their prayer lives become self-seeking and nearsighted. They are able to see the splinters in their brothers' eyes, but are unable to see the beams in their own eyes. They see the faults of others while they fail to see their own. They then become critical, censoring and condemning others while condoning themselves.

Someone has written, "When I'm prayed up-to-date, the worst people look good to me. When I'm not prayed up-to-date, the best people look hypocritical to me." People are selfish because they do not pray. If you are unloving to others and are refusing to speak or forgive them, then you do not have a prayer life. You can point the finger at someone else, but it is you that does not have a prayer life.

We can lose the spirit of love and compassion that we used to have. When you were first saved, you wanted everybody to be saved. You wanted everybody to be helped. You wanted everybody to be right. That was your desire, but something happened over time. You lost your compassion because you did not desire to be with the One Who is all-compassionate.

Why should the Lord give spiritual power to prayerless Christians? Why should He bless the prayerless with crowning victories? Why should the Lord give holy desires to those who come short in their prayer lives? You are not going to have the right desires if you do not pray, and you are not going to have compassion on others if you do not pray.

Successful Christian lives are contingent upon having victorious prayer lives. Without successful prayer lives, our Christianity will not amount to much. God will not bless us, and we cannot have revival. Doors will not open, and rivers of joy will not flow through our souls. It is easy to discern why some people are critical and do not possess a compassionate spirit or carry a burden for souls. It is easy to understand why they do not echo the question, *Is there not a cause?* Solomon said that *the curse causeless shall not come.* We know that there is a cause, but there is also a lack of prayer. Make prayer a reality in your life.

How much are you going to pray? I am weary of people who just play church. I spend hours in prayer, and I have given my whole life to do something for God. I do not have much time left, but I am going to give it all that I have. I am not playing the role of the little reverend. I am on a mission sent from God. We must do God's work. We need to help everybody we can to be saved. We need to save this country. We must get real about praying. My prayers alone are not going to do it. It is time that we realize the seriousness of the hour.

Are you suffering loss today? Is your life being blessed? Quit worrying about what you are going to do and start praying. Everybody is always wondering what he can do for the church. Get real about prayer! This subject should grab ahold of our heart. Will you not pray for your children or your grandchildren? Will you not pray for those you love? Will you not pray for your country?

CHAPTER 11

Developing a Greater Capacity for Answered Prayer

Psalms 66:18 states, *If I regard iniquity in my heart, the Lord will not hear me: But verily God hath heard me; he hath attended to the voice of my prayer. Blessed be God, which hath not turned away my prayer, nor his mercy from me.*

The Lord has heard and answered many of my prayers, but I want Him to answer many more. I want Him to answer mighty requests. God's promises and His commandments go hand in hand. We could say that they run parallel to each other. God has promised us many things in His Word. If we want what He has promised, we must obey His commandments. The Bible says that there is *no variableness, neither shadow of turning* with God. He will not change that which He has promised.

When the conditions of His promises are met, He will keep His Word. We need to determine the conditions that will move God to answer our prayers. Let us look at Scripture to examine several things we can do that will encourage God to listen and answer our prayers.

First, tithe off of all your income. Malachi 3:10-11 says, *Bring ye all the tithes into the storehouse, that there may be meat in mine house, and prove me now herewith, saith the LORD of hosts, if I will not open you the windows of heaven, and pour you out a blessing, that there shall not be room enough to receive it. And I will rebuke the devourer for your sakes, and he shall not destroy the fruits of your ground; neither shall your vine cast her fruit before the time in the field, saith the LORD of hosts.* Here is a wonderful promise. God says that He will open the windows of Heaven and pour out a blessing so great that you cannot receive it all. In addition, He says that He will protect you and bless your fruit. Things that would otherwise be devoured will be protected. What a wonderful promise!

This promise is a challenge to all of us. The Lord says in this passage, *prove me*. I like that. God is pleased when we obey Him, believe Him, and take Him at His Word. In this Scripture, God challenges us and gives us a legal right to prove Him.

When you make a promise to your children, they expect you to keep your word. When they have been promised a reward that will be given upon completion of a task, they will dedicate themselves to completing that task. When they are finished, they will report back to you, expecting the prize. If you are just, you will give them what you promised.

We go to the Lord when we have special needs in our lives. Our needs may be physical, material, or spiritual needs. We can look up to the Lord with courage and confidence and say, "Lord, I gave my tithes and offerings joyfully. I gave them willingly and cheerfully to You. You said to prove myself to You. I want You to prove Yourself to me." Do you know what God says that He will do? He will prove Himself and will keep His Word.

God wants to answer our prayers. He gives us special promises so that we can get greater prayers answered. He will bless you if you sacrifice and give yourself to Him. This promise is practical. Do not believe that He will let you suffer if you faithfully tithe and give your offerings to Him. He says, "I want you to prove yourself to Me. I will bless you and give you what you need." When you need help, you will be able to look to Him and say, "Lord, I want to remind You that I believed You. I joyfully gave, and now I am trusting You."

Secondly, live in God's purpose. Romans 8:28 says, *And we know that all things work together for good to them that love God, to them who are the called according to his purpose.* It has been said that "God's promises hang over His purposes." We want to show God that we love Him fervently, and the Bible says that the way to show love to Him is through our obedience.

God has a purpose for every day and every hour of the life that He gives you. He wants you to find that purpose and strive to do all that you can do to fulfill it. If you are living in His will and striving to fulfill His purpose, He has promised to supply your needs. Is that not a wonderful promise? God does not leave you out on a limb by yourself. God has a purpose for you. Find that purpose and give your life to it. You will discover that as you give your life to His purpose, He will supply whatever you need.

And we know that all things work together for good to them that love God, to them who are the called according to his purpose. Seeing God at work in our lives gives us courage and boldness in faith and prayer as we live for Him. God gives us the means to get all that He has out of Heaven. He promises us that He will do the hard part with His infinite power since He knows that we are weak. He wants us to accomplish what He has asked.

If God calls you to do something, He will give you what you need to do the job. What a wonderful thing to think about! If you are living in His purpose, you have the promise of God. If you call on Him, He will give you what you need to be a success. It does not matter how inadequate you feel. You need to strive to live in His purpose. Do what God has made you to do and fulfill what He has called you to do. If you do these things, He has promised that He will give you what you need. What a wonderful promise! What a wonderful God!

Thirdly, seek God's glory. Exodus 32:10 says, *Now therefore let me alone, that my wrath may wax hot against them, and that I may consume them: and I will make of thee a great nation.* Greatness is dangerous because most people cannot stand firm with either great material prosperity or spiritual success. People who start with apparent spiritual success have to be careful because they often digress quickly.

Talents have a tendency to cause a person to become prideful. Highly gifted people can easily begin to rely on their talent, leading them to self-trust, self-reliance, and pride. *Pride goeth before destruction.* The person who seeks to glorify God rather than himself will reach great heights, but many great men have fallen when seeking glory for themselves. They lost the glory of God. The greatness of mighty men of God lies in seeking glory only for Him.

Moses was a great example. He did not seek glory for himself, but he was dedicated to glorifying God and His name. As a result, he could move God and command Him so that He hearkened to his pleas. God could not say *no* to Moses because Moses was promoting only God's glory.

Can you imagine Deity crying out to humanity, "Leave me alone!" That is what God said to Moses. Could you get God to say that to you? God was saying to leave Him alone because God could not say *no* to Moses. Would it not be wonderful to have a prayer life where God could not say *no* to you. Moses did not leave God alone. He considered matters from God's viewpoint. Forgetting himself, he sought God's glory and the good of others. He employed that as a lever to pressure God, and God hearkened to him.

That is the power of prayer. If you pray for something, give God the glory for it. You do not have anything because of yourself; everything we have is because of Christ. All of the goodness and opportunities that we have come from our wonderful Saviour. When everything that we do is for His glory, God knows that He can trust us; and our relationship with Him will be such that He will not say *no* to us. What a wonderful thing! As we learn to seek His glory, we can get our prayers answered in a much greater way.

Fourthly, consider the poor. Psalms 41:1-3 says, *Blessed is he that considereth the poor: the LORD will deliver him in time of trouble. The LORD will preserve him, and keep him alive; and he shall be blessed upon the earth: and thou wilt not deliver him unto the will of his enemies. The LORD will strengthen him upon the bed of languishing: thou wilt make all his bed in his sickness.* Many times these verses are overlooked as if they were not in the Bible. If you consider the poor as this Scripture advises, this promise is good to plead before the Lord when physical needs arise. It will move God to bring deliverance in times of trouble. The Lord may preserve the one who considers the poor; for he is profitable, not only to God, but also to others.

If you practice this Scripture throughout your life, it will be a comfort to you in the eve of your life. You will have an easier time when your sun is setting. Some people experience a more difficult time than others when dying because they look back on their lives and see darkness. There is little satisfaction in what they have done for others. When they look into the future, there is darkness there too. They do not want to die and leave all their treasures to others.

The Bible says that if I give my life and treasure to others and live to please Him, I will have a life that is full of glory. When I reach my last days, I will be able to look back on my life and see how God has blessed and used me. I will also be able to look into the future and see the greater glory that awaits. We can die in peace remembering the promises of the Word of God and knowing that our treasures are laid up in Heaven and will be enjoyed forever. May we remember these wonderful promises of God!

We may languish on beds of sickness, but He promises He will bless us and watch over us while we are sick. It is all related to prayer. All parts of our lives, physical and spiritual, are bound in prayer. Prayer is the secret key to a successful life.

Fifthly, seek the welfare of others. Luke 11:8-9 says, *I say unto you, Though he will not rise and give him, because he is his friend, yet because of his importunity he will rise and give him as many as he* *needeth. And I say unto you, Ask, and it shall be given you; seek, and ye shall find; knock, and it shall be opened unto you.* A spiritually aggressive Christian can come with greater courage to the Lord. When he comes to the Lord on the behalf of another, He can press the claim harder and exercise more faith. You may feel a little intimidated when you pray for yourself, but you should be willing to press the Lord long and loud when you are praying for others.

We need to realize the opportunity we have in praying for others. We should have more confidence in praying for others than we do for ourselves. We ought to exercise more faith in God when we pray for others. Do not give up on praying for other people. Come boldly to the Throne of Grace, and plead for their needs. Pray and ask the Lord to help and bless them.

We read in this passage of the man who sought the welfare of another. He prayed repeatedly for bread for his friend, and he got it. We need to study the Bible and come to the place where we pray more powerfully and earnestly for others. When we plead for others, God says that He will bless us and answer those prayers. We live like spiritual paupers simply because we have not given God any prayers to answer. God wants to answer our prayers; we just have to ask Him.

Sixthly, walk before God with a perfect heart. Isaiah 38:2 and 3 says, *Then Hezekiah turned his face toward the wall,* *and prayed unto the* LORD, *And said, Remember now,* O LORD, *I beseech thee, how I have walked before thee in truth and with a perfect heart, and have done that which is good in thy sight. And Hezekiah wept sore.* Isaiah had come with a very startling message from the Lord. He told Hezekiah to get his house in order because he was going to die. Hezekiah began to pray. He wanted to live longer, and he knew that God was the only One Who could help him. He asked for a new lease on life. As leverage in getting his prayer answered, he reminded the Lord that he had walked before Him with a perfect heart. What happened? God answered his prayer and gave Hezekiah fifteen additional years.

Walking before God with a perfect heart and doing what is right in His sight will have a great weight in moving God to answer our prayers. We pray for our physical health, spiritual health, success in service, and material needs, and many scriptures have spiritual, physical, and material applications. Some address individuals, while others address groups or nations. The applications may be present or future. Remember that what Christ has done for others also applies to us. If we come to God with a perfect heart and a pure motive and serve Him with our life, we can confidently ask Him to answer our prayers. The implication of this Scripture is that God looks at our heart before answering our prayers. Stay close to God by walking and talking with Him; hence, He will answer our prayers.

Seventhly, pray for the things for which Christ prayed. When we are praying with Jesus for the things He desires, our prayer lives will be enhanced. Matthew 6:9-10 says, *After this manner therefore pray ye: Our Father which art in heaven, Hallowed be thy name. Thy kingdom come. Thy will be done in earth, as it is in heaven.* Jesus told the disciples to pray, *Thy kingdom come.* The coming of the Kingdom of God with a new Heaven and a new earth is a certainty. Do you pray for the Second Coming of Christ? One of these days, Jesus is going to step out on the clouds and say, "Come up hither." What is going to happen then? We are going up!

The dead in Christ shall rise first: Then we which are alive and remain shall be caught up together with them in the clouds, to meet the Lord in the air: and so shall we ever be with the Lord. We will ever be with the Lord! We ought to be praying for that day. The Bible says to *Pray for the peace of Jerusalem.* Pray for that day when Jesus shall reign, and we shall see His kingdom here on earth as He promised. We will see a new Heaven and new earth created. We will see that city coming down from God, the new Jerusalem. Our prayers will encourage the Lord to bring this time to pass as He has promised.

Luke 10:2 says, *Therefore said he unto them, The harvest truly is great, but the labourers are few: pray ye therefore the Lord of the harvest, that he would send forth labourers into his harvest.* We want to see as many people saved as possible. We share this desire with Jesus. Jesus said that we are to pray for laborers. He did not say to pray for souls to be saved. He said to pray for laborers. If laborers deliver His Gospel message, souls will be saved.

A good illustration of the result of praying for God's desires is seen in the release of the Jews from the seventy years of captivity in Babylon. Jeremiah prophesied the seventy years of captivity and subsequent release. God promised to do this. How did He accomplish it? He did it through the prayers and influence of Daniel. When God wants to bring something to pass, He uses a human instrument. Daniel prayed and was faithful, and God was encouraged by the prayers of Daniel.

Daniel had studied the prophecies of Jeremiah. He read the prediction of the release, and he became greatly burdened about it. In Daniel Chapter 9, you can read Daniel's prayer. He knew God's will and prayed for its fulfillment. His prayer acted to move God to bring it to pass. We can always remind God of what He has told us to do. "God, You told us to pray for laborers. We are praying for laborers, and we want the world to hear the Gospel." We should remind God that we are praying for His will to be done. That will give us a greater capacity to get our needs met.

It is the purpose of Jesus to evangelize the world through His followers. As a Christian, you should feel an individual responsibility. You should pray as if the salvation of others depended upon your prayers. Believe as if others depended upon your faith. Give as if God's work depended upon your giving. When we learn to have this kind of zeal, we will have taken on the true spirit of missions; and the world can be evangelized.

If we want revival in our generation, we have to come to the place where we work and pray as if it all depends on us. We do not have time to play around. We must be serious about the fact that the world is perishing. We need to pray as if revival in our nation depends on us. We should work as if the world is depending on us to save it. We need to fight Satan as if his defeat depended on us. We must do all that we can.

If we have done all we can do, we can look up to Heaven and ask God to help deliver us. We can ask Him to give us what we need, and He will do it. We need to ask Him for the laborers and pray for them so that His cause can be accomplished.

Jesus wants us to pray with devoutness. As you pray, you need to have your mind and heart right and possess the right words. When you come into His presence, realize that you are but ashes and dust. These are some things that we can do to improve our prayer lives.

We need to understand that when we pray, we are praying for the things that God desires. We can also ask for our petitions. When we pray prayers that He wants us to pray, we will see the Lord bless us and answer our prayers. Let us not just learn about prayer. Let us get answers to prayer. Let us put into practice what we are learning. May God help us to pray!

CHAPTER 12
Essentials for Effective Praying

James 5:16 says, *Confess your faults one to another, and pray one for another, that ye may be healed. The effectual fervent prayer of a righteous man availeth much.*

Prayer must be effective, yet most of our prayers do not qualify as such. Today, we seldom pray or preach with fervency. Fervency means "to be hot with the heat coming from the power of the Holy Spirit." Fervency is evidence of His presence in our prayer lives. *The effectual fervent prayer of a righteous man availeth much.*

All of us should strive to be effective in our praying. Many people say that they are praying; but, as we have seen from the Word of God, most of it is not really prayer. Most of our prayers are just praying and talking to ourselves, just as the Pharisee's prayer. We should have a desire in our heart to become effective in our prayer lives.

We often talk about growth in our Christian lives. Growth is an important element of our prayer lives. We should not be praying as we did when we first got saved. Our prayers should be of greater length. We should be praying for more things and seeing more answers to our prayers as we grow in the Lord Jesus Christ.

There are seven elements that you should consider in increasing the effectiveness of your prayers. As a Christian, you should work to incorporate these elements into your prayer life. As you integrate the following principles into your life, you will be able to observe an increase in your prayers' effectiveness. As Christians, we should be continuously growing in our praying ability.

First: Obedience to God's Commandments. I John 3:22 states, *And whatsoever we ask, we receive of him, because we keep his commandments, and do those things that are pleasing in his sight.*

This verse starts with *And whatsoever we ask, we receive of him, because we keep his commandments.* As we are keeping His commandments, we also *do those things that are pleasing in his sight.* This verse is straightforward. I can have whatever I ask of Him if I am willing to obey His commandments and do those things that are pleasing to Him. We must ask ourselves if we are meeting the criteria of this verse.

As a Christian, growing in our prayer life and receiving answers to our prayers are contingent upon our obedience to God. If we are obedient to Him, we can have answers to prayer. If we choose to disobey Him, we cannot have answers to prayer. It is as simple as that.

Some people have the idea that they can live any way that they want to live, and God will still hear and answer their prayers. However, the Bible tells us that He will not. A constant and persistent prayer life will have a great bearing on our victory, on our joy, and on our usefulness. However, God will not listen and answer our prayers if His commandments are not obeyed. If you are not going to obey and try to live for Him, you are wasting your time waiting for God to do something mighty for you.

Keep His simple commandments, and do those things that are pleasing in His sight. That is the way to have an effective prayer life. When you are doing your best to please Him and to obey His Word, His ears will be open to your prayers.

Second: Submission to God's Will. I John 5:14 says, *And this is the confidence that we have in him, that, if we ask any thing according to his will, he heareth us.*

Luke 22:41-42 says, *And he was withdrawn from them about a stone's cast, and kneeled down, and prayed, Saying, Father, if thou be willing, remove this cup from me: nevertheless not my will, but thine, be done.* Jesus was praying in the Garden of Gethsemane. He said, *if thou be willing.* We can ask anything according to His will and have confidence that He will hear us. Most of us have trouble doing this because we have made the will of God into something very complicated when it is not.

We cannot force God to do anything against His will. That is why we must look to Him in making decisions and in planning for our lives. Sometimes we think that we have the right to determine God's will for our life. You and I do not have the right to determine God's will for our lives. Nevertheless, we sometimes say, "I feel like this is the will of God." Well, I have news for you! Your feelings about the will of God are not worth anything. We are not Charismatics, and the will of God is not based on how we feel. Before there was a flower or a bird or a tree, God created you in His mind. He created you and predetermined a will for your existence. God did not just put you down here and suddenly say, "Well, how did he get there?" God has a will for your life. He placed you here on this earth to fulfill that will. You must be diligent in searching for God's will for your life, not your will. You cannot determine the will of God by feelings or emotions. God has a will for you, and it is your responsibility to find it.

When we find the will of God and live by His will, we can have confidence that He will give us whatever we ask. We must let Him plan our lives. When our will conforms to His will, He will let us have our will. It is not a matter of what you want or what you feel is the will of God. He says that when you conform to the will that He has planned for you and put it into practice in your life, He will let you have your will because it is His will. If we want what God wants us to have, we can have what we want. God is not hard to please when we want to please Him.

One of the greatest missions of our lives is to submit ourselves to the will of God. We can find His will in the Word of God. We have seen in these studies that you cannot have a prayer life without the Word of God. In order to have a good Christian life, we need to read and submit to the Word of God. Do what the Word of God leads you to do; and let God, through His Word, shape and mold your life. You will then find yourself doing the will of God.

We cannot wish for anything better than God's will for us. I wish Christians would understand that. Some Christians say, "Well, this is what I want to do. I just think this is better." How can you find anything better than that for which God created you? He put you here for a reason. God planned a life for you that will glorify and honor Him. If you will follow His plan, you will be happy as you rejoice at the Judgment Seat of Christ. Do you think you can find something better than what He has planned for you? You cannot! It is impossible! When you know that something is not according to His will for your life, you should not pray for it.

Praying in His will increases our faith and eliminates our doubts. We sometimes doubt for what we are asking because we are not sure if it is the will of God. We should not be constantly praying, "If it be Thy will." Many people do, and it means that they are doubting. They cannot say with confidence that they are praying for God's will. When you say, "If it be Thy will," you are really saying, "I don't really know Your will. What is Your will, God?" As you are searching for His will, there may be times when it is appropriate; but, in order to have effective prayer lives, we must pray in His will.

We should go to the Bible to find His will. His will cannot be found in some religious experience. You can find His will when the Holy Spirit gives you comfort and assurance that it is the right thing based on your study of the Word of God. There are some things that we know are His will, such as salvation of sinners and promises in His Word.

Fervent prayers incite conflict that demands faith and courage. When we know something is God's will, we can ask Him for it with courage and faith. Submission to God's will is a condition necessary for prayers to be answered.

Third: Humility of Character. II Chronicles 7:14 states, *If my people, which are called by my name, shall humble themselves, and pray, and seek my face, and turn from their wicked ways; then will I hear from heaven, and will forgive their sin, and will heal their land.*

Some Christians say, "Pray for me. I have a problem with pride." If you have a problem with pride, do something about it. Nobody can do anything about your pride but you. Nobody can do anything about your spirit but you. The Bible instructs you to humble yourself.

The Scripture tells God's people to *humble themselves and pray*. First, you must humble yourself, and then you can pray. We often run to pray without humbling ourselves. We come in with pride, but God says that He *resisteth the proud*. If we do not humble ourselves, our prayers will not be answered; and God will not give us that for which we ask.

This verse continues in instructing those who are humbly praying to *seek my face, and turn from their wicked ways; then will I hear from heaven, and will forgive their sin, and will heal their land*. That is a wonderful promise! Christians say they are praying for revival, and they wonder what is wrong with God. Nothing is wrong with God; we are the problem. He tells us to humble ourselves, to pray, to seek His face, and to turn from our wicked ways. When we have done all of these, He will then hear.

We must realize that we need humility of character. We need to be free from pride and arrogance. Only when we realize that we are unworthy of God can we truly be humble. Humility should be a character trait of a Christian; however, it should never be regarded as inadequacy. Abraham came before God and said he was but *dust and ashes.* That is all—just dust and ashes. Isaiah tells us that our very best, our righteousness, is like a pile of old, putrid, filthy rags when placed before the Lord. I have nothing to bring to God. I have nothing to offer to God but a humble spirit for Him to use as He desires.

Humility of heart greatly moves God. Nothing will draw as much promotion and exaltation from God as our humility. It draws God down to us and moves Him to place His arm underneath us and lift us up. James said, *Humble yourselves in the sight of the Lord, and he shall lift you up.* Do you want to be lifted up? Humble yourself. Do you want God to answer your prayers? Humble yourself.

Humility not only brings promotion but also moves God to do as we ask in our prayers. Peter said, *Humble yourselves therefore under the mighty hand of God, that he may exalt you in due time.* Continuously humble yourself so that He can exalt you when the time is right. If you make an appeal to God with humility of heart and life, you have a promise that He will hear you. God is not going to hear someone who has a proud and self-sufficient spirit because God says that He resists the proud. If you are full of pride, you can pray all you want; but God will resist you and your prayers.

Fourth: Holiness of Heart and Life. I Timothy 2:8 says, *I will therefore that men pray every where, lifting up holy hands, without wrath and doubting.* We need holiness in our lives.

Holiness is Godlikeness. It is a moral attribute of God that involves the will. God wills us to be holy and is greatly pleased with His children who are holy. We are commanded to follow and seek after holiness as an experience and as a practice.

Holiness begins with regeneration when we get saved. At that time, the character of Christ is imparted to us as we are born again. Holiness continues in our lives through sanctification as we are set apart for Heaven. We are set apart for holiness in our lives. We are set apart for His service. Holiness will be consummated in glorification when I am in His presence and just as He is.

When our lives are holy, God is greatly pleased. If we want our prayers answered, we must follow after holiness. We must make a decision. Will we strive to live our lives holy like Christ, or will we choose to live sinful lives?

If you choose a sinful life, it means that there will be no answers to your prayers. You will be cutting off fellowship and communion with God. It means that you can get someone else to pray for you, but your prayers will not get through. You can light candles all day long, but you will not get answers to your prayers. If you choose sin over righteousness and holiness, you can do whatever you want; but God will not accept you or your prayers.

Fifth: Fervency of Spirit. James 5:16 states, *Confess your faults one to another, and pray one for another, that ye may be healed. The effectual fervent prayer of a righteous man availeth much.* Someone once said the following words:

> It is not the arithmetic of our prayers, how many there are; nor the rhetoric of our prayers, how elegant they be; nor the geometry of our prayers, how long they may be; nor the music of our prayers, how sweet our voice may be; nor the logic of our prayers, how argumentative they may be; nor the method of our prayers, how orderly they may be; nor the divinity of our prayers, how good the doctrine may be which God cares for.

The effectual fervent prayer of a righteous man availeth much. An effectual prayer is an energetic prayer. A prayer that has been wrought and breathed by the Holy Spirit is hot. Fervent means "to boil, to be hot." One thing we need today is fervent prayer.

When was the last time you cried when you prayed because your heart was broken? When was the last time you were fervent in your prayers? When was the last time you shed tears as you prayed because of the urgency of your requests? When was the last time that you fervently poured out your soul to God?

We need fervent prayer and fervent preaching today. Everything today is lukewarm. Nobody wants to get worked up. When we pray, we need to realize that we are really having a personal encounter with God.

The effectual prayer must be both human and divine. The fervor of the Christian and the fervor of the Holy Spirit join together as they plead in earnest, the human heart having been set ablaze by the fire of the Holy Spirit. Such a prayer will go through to the Throne of Grace. It is a prayer within a prayer.

The Bible says that the Holy Spirit is our prayer partner. It says that He prays with us. When we do not know what to say in prayer, He will say the words for us. If we make Him our prayer partner, He will ask God to give us what we need. I want my prayers to be answered. As my prayer partner, He can help me to know what to pray for because He knows what God wants and how God wants to work in my life. When He is my prayer partner, my prayer will go to Heaven as a prayer within a prayer. God is answering not only my prayer but also the prayer of the Holy Spirit. The Holy Spirit will take my prayer with Him into the throne room of God.

James said that *Elias* [Elijah] *was a man subject to like passions as we are, and he prayed earnestly*. The prayer within a prayer has a power that carries the petition to God, and nothing can stop it from going through. Oh, how we need to be filled with the Holy Spirit and need to invoke Him as our prayer partner! Too often, we just rush our prayers and very glibly spew out some words. We do not take time to be holy. We do not take time to meditate on the Word of God. We do not take time to let God help us.

What a way for us to get our prayers answered! If we have the Holy Spirit as our prayer partner, we can pray in confidence because our prayers go together right into the presence of God. What a wonderful thing to know!

Sixth: Regularity in Prayer. In Psalms 55:17 we find, *Evening, and morning, and at noon, will I pray, and cry aloud: and he shall hear my voice.* David was praying three times a day, and he said that God would hear his voice. It is important to have regular places that you meet with God and regular times scheduled for your prayer life. These times should not be haphazard. Evening is mentioned first because the Jews started each day at sunset.

Daniel 6:10 says, *Now when Daniel knew that the writing was signed* [prohibiting prayer to other than the king], *he went into his house; and his windows being open in his chamber toward Jerusalem, he kneeled upon his knees three times a day, and prayed, and gave thanks before his God, as he did aforetime.* The Bible speaks of this so many times that it should draw our attention. Three times a day is a good number of times to pray. Both David and Daniel are documented as having prayed in the evening, morning, and at noon. They knew that God would answer their prayers.

Do you want answers to your prayers? If the Bible said, "If you stand on your head, God will answer your prayers," would you stand on your head? I am sure that I would need help, but I would do my best to comply because I want God to answer my prayers. If He says to pray three times a day, I think that I will do that. He says to make the Holy Spirit my prayer partner, so I think I will do that too.

This is all about getting our prayers answered. If God answers prayer, why are we in such a mess? We are not getting our prayers answered because we do not do what the Bible tells us to do. We do what we think is right in our own eyes. Notice that Daniel had a regular place to pray. It was always in the same place with the window open. He had a regular prayer position. He got down on his knees. He had a petition that he prayed and a number of times that he prayed. He was prepared to pray. It was not something that he just happened to do. When he went to pray, he did not say, "Oh, dear God, save me from the lion's den." He prayed as if there were no lion's den. He prayed as he always did. He prayed with regularity.

When we pray, God takes the regularity of our prayer lives into consideration. The person who is irregular in his prayer life, praying only on occasion or when he has an emergency, should not expect answers to his prayers. Many people pray only when they have trouble, and then they quit. God is not going to answer their prayers. He may answer the prayers of others who are praying for them, but it is not an answer to their prayers. God is moved to answer our prayers when our regular prayer lives are consistent with our objectives and motives. Your prayer life can be more effective if you are a person who prays regularly.

Seventh: Faith in God and His Promises. Matthew 21:22 says, *And all things, whatsoever ye shall ask in prayer, believing, ye shall receive.* The word *all* does not omit anything, does it? If I *ask in prayer, believing,* then I can receive. We honor God when we believe in His goodness, greatness, and generosity. We cannot honor or please God in any greater way than by believing what He has promised. We need to bring our petitions to God, both small and large. Our faith in God pleases Him, and moves Him to answer our prayers.

Where do we get the words to pray? We get them from the Bible. If you do not read your Bible, you do not even know how to pray. To have words to pray, you must get them from the Bible. When I find something in the Bible that God has promised, I claim it and ask Him to honor that promise based on His Word. He has to do it.

If God answers prayer, why are we in such a mess? You may talk about answered prayers, but do you really have those answers? If you are not saved, you cannot pray. You can be religious and pretend to pray, but you have to be born again and become a part of the family before you can ask anything of the Father.

The only prayer a lost person can pray that will be heard is the sinner's prayer. If you are saved and know you are living in sin, you cannot get answers to your prayers. If you are saved and you doubt God, you cannot get answers to your prayers. You cannot get answers to your prayers until you believe the Bible. Start following the Book, and you can have answered prayer.

Prayer is the secret to the Christian life. The only way that you can have a prayer life is through the Bible. The Bible is our prayer book. It has all the instruction and direction we need to get the answers to our prayers. If you want things in your life, why not do something about getting them?

You have lost loved ones. Who is going to pray for them? You know people who are away from God, facing His judgment. Who is going to pray for them? You have great needs in your life. Who is going to pray for them? Who is going to pray for your husband, your wife, and your children? Who is going to pray for our country if you do not? Get a prayer life!

If you know you cannot pray, be honest about it and get it right. If you cannot pray because of pride, humble yourself so God can do something for you. Realize that you are not as good or important as you think you are. Realize that you are nothing but *dust and ashes*. If Abraham believed that about himself, then why should you not believe the same about yourself? If Isaiah believed that *all our righteousnesses are as filthy rags*, then why should we believe differently? Paul said, *when I would do good, evil is present with me.* He said that there is a battle raging. He said that he was a servant to whomever he yielded himself. Some yield to the world and the flesh; others yield to God. Realizing this, we must make sure that we are right with God.

Somebody's life can be changed if you get a prayer life. Somebody's world can be saved if you learn to pray. If you will enter into His presence in prayer, you can have the sweetest fellowship with the Lord that you have ever known.

CHAPTER 13

The Locking and Unlocking Power of Prayer

James 5:17-18 says, *Elias* [Elijah] *was a man subject to like passions as we are, and he prayed earnestly that it might not rain: and it rained not on the earth by the space of three years and six months. And he prayed again, and the heaven gave rain, and the earth brought forth her fruit.* In verse 17, we see Elijah praying and locking up the heavens. For three years and six months, it did not rain because of the prayer of Elijah. Then, in verse 18, he prayed again; and it was by that prayer that the heavens were opened and the rains came. This is not just a recounting of one man's prayer life. In this passage of Scripture, we find truths that apply to everyone's prayer life.

There is a locking and unlocking power of prayer. Prayer can prevent things; and, conversely, it can cause things to happen. When we develop a powerful prayer life, we can do miraculous things. We may or may not be able to keep it from raining, but there are people whom we can reach and help. If we learn to pray as God has instructed, our homes and land can be healed.

It has been said that prayer is the key that locks and unlocks Heaven's door. Heaven is the source of God's blessings. If you call on God, He will issue forth those *great and mighty things, which thou knowest not.* Prayer is the key that opens all of His blessings to you.

A key is an instrument to move the bolt of a lock which causes it lock or unlock. The word *key* may also be defined as "a term to solve or explain some problem, condition, or situation." A lock only functions with the use of a matching key, and the key that opens one door will not open other doors.

Heaven is spoken of as a place having windows, doors, and gates. Prevailing prayer, coupled with faith, is the right key to open Heaven's doors and release the blessings of God. Many things come to pass as we pray, yet many things have not come to pass because of missed opportunities to pray. When we get to Heaven, we will find that we missed many blessings simply because we did not ask God for them. We will also find that many things we thought we had accomplished by our own power were only fulfilled as a result of answered prayer. Prayer and faith form a key that opens the doors and windows of Heaven. From those windows, God showers His blessings upon us. We will furthur discuss some Biblical examples of the locking and unlocking power of prayer.

First, by prayer, Moses unlocked the Red Sea. Exodus 14:15-16 says, *And the LORD said unto Moses, Wherefore criest thou unto me? speak unto the children of Israel, that they go forward: But lift thou up thy rod, and stretch out thine hand over the sea, and divide it: and the children of Israel shall go on dry ground through the midst of the sea.* At this time, Moses had already led the children of Israel out of Egypt, and they had gone out into the wilderness by way of the Red Sea. They came to a place in their travel where they were hemmed in by rocks and hills on one side. The Red Sea was in front of them, and Pharaoh and his army were behind them. The children of Israel became afraid because there appeared to be no way out. If they went into the Red Sea, they would drown. If they went back to Pharaoh, he would kill them. If they continued out into the wilderness, they could not live; and, even if they could survive the wilderness, Pharaoh would probably hunt them down and destroy them. What could they do?

They began to ask Moses about their predicament. Moses then used the key of faith and cried out to the Lord about the situation. God was moved by Moses' cry and said, "Moses, I have heard you. Tell the people to go forward." God made a highway directly through the sea, and the children of Israel went over on dry ground. Pharaoh and his army pursued them but perished on that highway as God returned the sea to its normal place after Moses and the children of Israel had passed through. This is a very good Biblical illustration of receiving the blessings of God by asking Him for them in prayer. Just as the children of Israel could not get to the other side of the sea on their own, you cannot get to God or Heaven by your own works or deeds. It has to be through the way that God provides. God provided a way out for the children of Israel. They followed by faith and were delivered.

Prayer has an unlocking power and makes a way when there is no way. Prayer and faith make things come to pass when it seems there is no help, no hope, nowhere to look, and no escape. That is why the Bible says, *Call unto me, and I will answer thee, and shew thee great and mighty things, which thou knowest not.* Do not believe for a minute that anything is impossible. We have the key! The key of faith and prayer can unlock the doors and windows of Heaven. This key will allow God to pour His blessings out upon us. What an illustration! Moses unlocked the Red Sea with prayer. He had the right key!

Secondly, by prayer, Elijah locked the heavens. James 5:17 says, *Elias* [Elijah] *was a man subject to like passions as we are, and he prayed earnestly that it might not rain: and it rained not on the earth by the space of three years and six months.* Elijah was a man of like passions. This means that he was just like you and me. We sometimes look at people in the Bible and picture them wearing a Superman outfit. We think that they had special powers given to them, but they were just like we are. Their every accomplishment and every miracle came about by prayer and faith. It is by faith, trust, and prayer that God has always worked.

In Israel, Ahab had insulted God by practicing idolatry. The Lord was provoked by this and revoked His blessings upon Israel. Elijah was the prophet whom God sent to Ahab with His startling message.

In his pride, King Ahab thought that he could do anything. He thought that he was invincible. When Ahab thought he had gotten away with everything, Elijah suddenly appeared. Of course, King Ahab was dumbfounded. I can see Elijah sticking his finger in Ahab's face and telling him, "You are the one who troubleth Israel." Then I can see Ahab retorting, "No, you are the one who troubleth Israel."

Then, Elijah took out that key and told Ahab that *As the LORD God of Israel liveth, before whom I stand, there shall not be dew nor rain these years, but according to my word.* Can you imagine how that shocked the king? He had been strutting high, illegally taking possesions, and murdering people. He had turned his back on God. The Bible tells us that the preacher showed up with his key. Elijah had the key that was shutting off the water.

The Bible says that as soon as Elijah had delivered his message, he was gone. Ahab looked everywhere for Elijah but could not find him. Ahab even sent search parties out to find him.

For three years and six months, there was no rain or dew in Israel. Ahab was so angry that he sought for Elijah everywhere. During that period of time, the heavens were locked up; however, God hid Elijah and took care of him.

Do not be afraid to use that key when God brings you to a door. Elijah could have protested, "If I do that, if I even say that, God, he will kill me." He did not say that but simply did just as the Lord instructed.

Do not be afraid to pray for anything for which you ought to pray. Some people say that we cannot have revival in this day and time. Well, why do we not just pray about it? Some say that God cannot work as He did in earlier days. God is still the same today as He was yesterday! We just need to get real about praying and talking to Him. Why can we not see? Elijah shut the heavens with the key.

Thirdly, by prayer, Elijah unlocked the heavens. James 5:18 says, *And he prayed again, and the heaven gave rain, and the earth brought forth her fruit.* The day came when Ahab was just walking down the road, and suddenly Elijah appeared. After three and a half years, here is that preacher right in Ahab's face. Bypassing all the king's guards and sentries, Elijah appeared on the scene. Take note of his boldness. If you have the key, you can be bold. Elijah said, "It's time to settle this thing. We are going to demonstrate that the God of Abraham, Isaac, and Israel is God. He shall prove Himself by fire." The people had to acknowledge God, for we know the contest that took place. We know how Elijah prayed, and the fire came down and destroyed all the sacrifices, licking up the water that was in the trenches. The people began to shout, *The LORD, he is the God; the LORD, he is the God.*

The time then came for the heavens to be opened for rain. Elijah stood and took the same key he had used to close up the heavens as he began to pray. The Bible says that Elijah had to pray seven times before they spotted a cloud bringing rain.

This should encourage us to use the key of prayer. Elijah was a man like we are. He kept praying earnestly, and the rain came. Our problem is that we do not think our key works, and we give up after only one try. One of the most humbling things in the world is when you constantly complain about your key not working, and someone comes along and shows you how to use it correctly.

We pray once; and if we do not get an instant response, we think that it does not work. Elijah had enough faith to pray seven times. I suspect that Ahab and his 850 prophets of Baal were getting excited when the first prayers brought no rain. They possibly thought that they were going to have another chance, but then the key worked.

Consider what we could do if we, like Elijah, would pray earnestly until the key worked. We get frustrated, walk off, and quit. There is nothing wrong with the key! You do not have to scheme. You can trust God to do what He says. Hold on to that key of prayer and faith.

Do not pray one time and say, "Oh well, it doesn't work." Do not pray two times and say the same thing. How long should you pray? If God told you to pray a certain number of times to get an answer, you would pray that many times. God wants you to pray as the old song says—"Just keep on praying 'till the light breaks through. The Lord will answer, He'll answer you." That is how God works.

Fourthly, by prayer, Daniel unlocked secrets. Daniel 2:17-19 says, *Then Daniel went to his house, and made the thing known to Hananiah, Mishael, and Azariah, his companions: That they would desire mercies of the God of heaven concerning this secret; that Daniel and his fellows should not perish with the rest of the wise men of Babylon. Then was the secret revealed unto Daniel in a night vision. Then Daniel blessed the God of heaven.* Daniel was another Bible character who was skillful in employing the key of prayer.

Daniel and his companions were to be put to death if they could not recount one of the king's dreams, a dream which the king, himself, had forgotten. That would be great, would it not? "Tell me what I dreamed and forgot, or I am going to kill you and your friends."

Facing this, they did not panic. They prayed, and God answered their prayers. God gave them the details of the king's dream and of its interpretation. As a result, their lives were spared.

They employed the key that unlocks secrets. God had given Nebuchadnezzar the dream, and then God caused him to forget it, leaving Nebuchadnezzar with a troubled mind. When Daniel and his friends prayed, God gave the answer to Daniel in his sleep. When he gave the answer to Nebuchadnezzar, Daniel was careful to give God the glory for revealing the dream and for applying it to Nebuchadnezzar's kingdom and future empires.

You may become frustrated, and there may be many things that you do not understand. The reason is that you do not use the right key. There are many things you cannot comprehend because you are defeated in your prayer life.

Do not continue down the road of trying to get a handle on things with the help of advisors and counselors, when all you need to do is put the key in and turn it. God says that He will reveal things to you as you enter into His presence in prayer. When you enter into the Holy of Holies as nothing but *dust and ashes*, humbling yourself before Him, Jeremiah 33:3 says that He will show you *great and mighty things.*

There are things that God wants to do for us in our lives that we do not even know. He wants to do things for our homes, for our children, for our churches, and for us personally.

Those things will not happen if we do not ask for them to happen. Think of some extreme thing that would be within God's will, but that you think He cannot do. Take the challenge of prayer, and see what God can do!

Fifthly, by prayer, Daniel locked the lions' mouths. Daniel 6:10 says, *Now when Daniel knew that the writing was signed, he went into his house; and his windows being open in his chamber toward Jerusalem, he kneeled upon his knees three times a day, and prayed, and gave thanks before his God, as he did aforetime.* Daniel made no pretense about it. When they prohibited praying to anyone but King Darius, what did he do? Three times a day, he went to the same place where he always prayed. With his windows opened, he knelt and prayed aloud. He prayed for God's blessing. He prayed his regular prayer *as he did aforetime.*

Daniel 6:22 says, *My God hath sent his angel, and hath shut the lions' mouths, that they have not hurt me: forasmuch as before him innocency was found in me; and also before thee, O king, have I done no hurt.* Daniel was a man of prayer. The most important thing in his life was prayer. He prayed three times a day and was, therefore, skillful in the employment of the key which unlocks secrets. We all know that because his faithfulness in prayer, Daniel was cast into the den of lions. There he was to become food for them, but he did not fear his enemies or the lions because he was faithful in his prayer life. Many fears that we have could be banished by a real prayer life.

I believe that Daniel had been in prayer for his preservation for many years. When he was taken away captive as a teenage boy by a wicked army, I am sure that he prayed for his preservation.

God shut the lions' mouths, and He locked their jaws so that they had a unique type of lockjaw. It is unscriptural to picture Daniel in the den with the lions' mouths open, preparing to devour him. Their mouths were already locked. I believe that when he hit the bottom of the lions' den, those lions may have thought that it was meal time; but they could not even open their mouths. They had no power because Daniel had the real power. He had the power of prayer and the power of trust and dependence on God. For Daniel, the prayer key was just as effective in locking the lions' mouths as it was in unlocking secrets. He was familiar with the use of that key and confident that it would work as it had many times before.

When Daniel was thrown into the lions' den, he did not have to spend an hour in prayer. He was thrown into the midst of many hungry lions. It was not the time to have to get right with God. Daniel said that they did not eat him because of his innocence. God saw the innocence in Daniel's heart; and, because of that innocence, God spared him. Daniel had purity of heart and mind because of the time he had spent in prayer. He was right with God before he faced the lions' den.

Most people need their prayers answered, but cannot get them answered because they first need to ask God to forgive them. They need to get their hearts right with God and to restore fellowship with the Heavenly Father.

We should always be ready and praying ahead of time. Daniel's prayers ahead of time availed him in his hour of persecution and possible death. Those who keep their hearts right can pray in an emergency. Their prayers go through immediately. The Bible says that *the effectual fervent prayer of a righteous man availeth much.*

What if Daniel had not been praying? He might have been angry at someone or had bitterness or lust in his heart. What if he had not been right with God when he was thrown into the lions' den? What would Daniel have done if he had not had the key to shut the lions' mouths? Would the lions have listened if he had called timeout? He would have been dead!

There are many situations that end tragically only because we do not pray. Who will be impacted because you are not praying for yourself, praying for others, and preparing for the evil day? The evil day is coming for all of us. We must prepare for it by having a prayer life.

Sixthly, by prayer, the early church unlocked the prison. Acts 12:5-10 says, *Peter therefore was kept in prison: but prayer* *was made without ceasing of the church unto God for him. And when Herod would have brought him forth, the same night Peter was sleeping between two soldiers, bound with two chains: and the keepers before the door kept the prison. And, behold, the angel of the Lord came upon him, and a light shined in the prison: and he smote Peter on the side, and raised him up, saying, Arise up quickly. And his chains fell off from his hands. And the angel said unto him, Gird thyself, and bind on thy sandals. And so he did. And he saith unto him, Cast thy garment about thee, and follow me. And he went out, and followed him; and wist not that it was true which was done by the angel; but thought he saw a vision. When they were past the first and the second ward, they came unto the iron gate that leadeth unto the city; which opened to them of his own accord: and they went out, and passed on through one street; and forthwith the angel departed from him.*

What a miraculous story! Herod had killed James with a sword. This made everybody, especially the Jews, so happy that Herod decided that he would kill Peter next. He cast Peter into prison and intended to kill him after the feast of the Jews. However, the Bible says that *prayer was made without ceasing of the church unto God for him.* I Thessalonians 5:17 tells us to *Pray without ceasing,* and that is what this church was doing. The night before Peter was to be executed, the prayer still had not been answered, but they kept on praying.

Then, God sent an angel to deliver Peter. When the angel came to get Peter, the angel had to wake Peter. Peter was sleeping! Could you sleep if you knew that they were scheduled to cut off your head the next day? I do not think I could.

This shows you something important about Peter. In spite of his lapse at Gethsemane, he was a man of prayer. He had put his situation in the Lord's hands. Peter knew that, if the Lord answered the church's prayer and got him out, he would live for Him. Hence, if he were not released but executed, then he would be in Heaven. Peter probably said to himself, "Well, I can't lose, so I think I will just take a nap."

When Perer was in prison bound to two soldiers, the angel awoke him; and the chains miraculoussly fell off. An unseen hand removed those chains. Then, as Peter began to move through the prison, the inner and the outer gates opened of their own accord.

Try to picture this! Peter was walking through the prison with the angel at his side. His chains had fallen off, and the gates were opening for him as he approached. He did not see anyone other than the angel who was with him. Nobody had to break them out or force the gates open because the gates were opening on their own!

The prayer of the church explains it all. The soldiers were asleep, but the saints of God were awake. Let us learn from this account that while the world sleeps and plays, we ought to be praying without ceasing. Therein lies our power!

The church prayed while the soldiers slept. Prayer proved to be stronger than the king. It was stronger than the prison and its chains, soldiers, gates, and locks.

Prayer is stronger than sin, and prayer is stronger than the devil himself! Do not tell me you cannot pray people out of trouble. You can! Every prison door has a lock, and the key of prayer can turn and open it. God's plan was to spare Peter through the prayers of His people. Praise the Lord for the prayers of the early church that unlocked that prison!

There used to be a time when churches got together and prayed for sinners, and sinners were saved. They prayed for backsliders, and backsliders got right with God. We are too busy to pray now. We go to church, but we want church to be a coffee shop. We want to be entertained and have all the frivolity of the world. We want church to be like a social club when it is supposed to be a hospital that rescues sinners. We need to realize that when we come to God's house, we should be burdened for people and their needs. We need to come to church to pray and ask God to do something.

Seventhly, by prayer, Paul and Silas unlocked the prison stocks. In Acts 16:25-26 we find, *And at midnight Paul and Silas prayed, and sang praises unto God: and the prisoners heard them. And suddenly there was a great earthquake, so that the foundations of the prison were shaken: and immediately all the doors were opened, and every one's bands were loosed.* Do you know why Paul and Silas were in prison? They were not in prison just for preaching, even though that was outwardly why they were put there. They were beaten and put in prison because the devil was trying to stop them. It was from this jail cell that the Gospel went to Europe, and from Europe, it came to America. This was a key event in the perpetuation of the Gospel of Jesus Christ by which we are saved!

Satan did not want the Gospel to go into Europe, and Paul and Silas were imprisoned in his attempt to stop them. Their bodies were beaten and bruised. Their feet were made fast in the stocks. They were not allowed to sleep or preach, but they could and did pray. When you cannot preach, you can pray. When you cannot sing, you can pray. When it seems that life, Satan, your weakness, and health have you bound so that you cannot move, you can pray! When you see no purpose or use for your life, you can pray! Midnight is just as good as any other time to pray because we have a God who never sleeps.

The subject of the prayers of Paul and Silas is not stated. We can only conjecture that they prayed for their enemies, for success, for guidance, for perseverance, for divine favor, for deliverance, and for the accomplishment of God's will. While these two men were praying, a third One was present. Remember, the Bible says, *For where two or three are gathered together in my name, there am I in the midst of them.* Do you want to feel close to the Lord? Why do you not pray? You might say that you just do not feel anything. The reason for this is that you do not pray.

As I mentioned earlier, there was somebody there with Paul and Silas. They were locked in a prison and bound in stocks, but they still prayed. By this time, you know what prayer can do. Suddenly the stocks and the prison doors were unlocked. This time, the answer came in the form of an earthquake. They prayed for deliverance, and God answered their prayer in an amusing manner.

God's reply was, "Okay, I will send you an earthquake." That would be somewhat scary! Are you not glad that God does not let you know how He is going to accomplish His will? God sent an earthquake, and it served as a key. They were free! Revival broke out in prison, and the preachers were set free. They then went to Europe and preached the Gospel. There it took root, grew, and spread.

God used these faithful men to preserve the Gospel, enabling it to be handed down from generation to generation. The Gospel came from a jail cell where two preachers were at a point that appeared as if all were lost, but then they prayed. When you begin to pray, you take out the key of faith; and God will open doors for you.

If God answers prayer, why are we in such a mess? If God answers prayer, why are our loved ones still lost? If God answers prayer, why are backsliders not being reclaimed? If God answers prayer, why do we not see revival? The answer has to be because we are not praying. We have the same God that those men had. The Bible says that God's hearing is still just as good. Isaiah said that *the LORD's hand is not shortened, that it cannot save.* He still has the same power and reach that He has always had, but our sins separate us from God and His power.

What stops a prayer life? Sin! It is very simple. That is why the Bible tells us not to even bother asking for revival until we do something about our own sin. The Bible tells us that when we come to the altar and have a problem with a brother, we must *first be reconciled to thy brother, and then come and offer thy gift.*

Do not ask God for anything until you first take care of your sin. If you do not take care of sin, you cannot use your key. Thank God that there is a key that unlocks Heaven, can roll back a sea, can open prison doors, and can even stop and start the rains. It is the key of prayer and faith. You have the key. Go use it! By faith, let God open doors for you and do great things!

To order additional copies please contact:

BEREAN PUBLICATIONS

A Ministry of Berean Baptist Church
4459 US Highway 17
Fleming Island, FL 32003
Phone: (904) 264-5333
Fax: (904) 264-9185
Email: info@bereanmail.org
www.thebereanbaptistchurch.com